GCSE BUSINESS STUDIES: THE ESSENTIALS

NEIL DENBY
PETER THOMAS

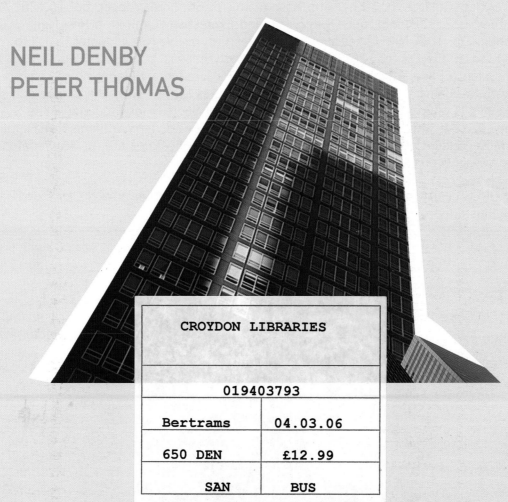

Hodder Arnold

A MEMBER OF THE HODDER HEADLINE GROUP

Acknowledgements

Thank you to my wife, Kath Thomas for inspiring the section openers for Sections 5 and 7.

Peter Thomas

The authors and publishers would like to thank the following institutions and individuals for permission to reproduce copyright illustrative material:

Action images, pp. 6, 8; The Advertising Archive, pp. 114, 120; Airbus, p. 58; Alex Livesay/Getty Images, p. 22; Alex Maguire/Rex Features Ltd, p. 49; Alix/Phanie/Rex Features Ltd, p. 136; Altrendo/Getty Images, p. 90; Andrew Mitchell, p. 55; Angela Hampton/Bubbles, p. 69; Anthony Bannister/Gallo/Corbis, p. 138; BP plc, p. 44; Britt Erlanson/Getty Images, p. 24; Bruce Ayres/Getty Images, p. 4; Bruno de Hoques/Getty Images, p. 57; Bulb Media Ltd./www.bulbmag.com, p. 48; Chuck Savage/Corbis, p. 32; Citroen, p. 73; Corbis/Reuters, p. 12; Corbis/© Walt Disney/Pixar Animation/Bureau L.A. Collections, p. 124; Dyson, p. 2; E.M. Welch/Rex Features Ltd, p. 92; Fairtrade Foundation, p. 132; Fredrick Renander/Alamy, p. 76; Getty Images, p. 14; Hornby Hobbies Ltd, p. 118; Ian Hodgson/Reuters/Corbis, p. 82; Ingram, p. 110; Inland Revenue, p. 30; Jack Sullivan/Alamy, p. 9; Jose Luis Pelaez, Inc/Corbis, p. 84; Jung Yeon-Ye/ Getty Images, p. 139; Justin Kase/Alamy, p. 64; Lorna Ainger, pp. 16, 26, 72, 90, 106, 111, 119, 122, 128; MFI, pp. 18, 52; Midland Expressway Limited, p. 47; Neil Tingle/Actionplus, p. 105; Nils Jorgensen/Rex Features Ltd, p. 87; Nissan Motor (GB) Ltd, p. 54; Noritsu (UK) Ltd, p. 86; O2, p. 126; Patrick Riviere/Getty Images, p. 36; 12; Paul Shambroom/Science Photo Library, p. 33; Photofusion Picture Library/Alamy, p. 17; The Photolibrary Wales/Alamy, p. 24; Richard Jones/Rex Features Ltd, p. 129; The photograph of KitKat packaging is reproduced with the kind permission of Société des Produits Nestlé S.A, p. 108; Sony, p. 134; Steve Forrest/Insight/Panos Pictures, p. 78; Terry Williams/Rex Features Ltd, p. 46; Tim Mosenfelder/Getty Images, p. 1; Tony Kyriacou/Rex Features Ltd, p. 36; Vodafone, pp. 80, 81; www.gner.co.uk, p. 42.

Artworks by Bill Greenhead and Mark Watkinson at Illustration. Further artworks by Oxford Designers & Illustrators.

Orders: please contact Bookpoint Ltd, 130 Milton Park, Abingdon, Oxon OX14 4SB. Telephone: (44) 01235 827720. Fax: (44) 01235 400454. Lines are open from 9.00–6.00, Monday to Saturday, with a 24-hour message answering service. You can also order through our website www.hoddereducation.co.uk

If you have any comments to make about this or any of our other titles, please send them to educationenquiries@hodder.co.uk
British Library Cataloguing in Publication Data
A catalogue record for this title is available from the British Library

ISBN-10: 0 340 88784 2
ISBN-13: 978 0 340 88784 4

Published 2005
Impression number   10 9 8 7 6 5 4 3 2 1
Year   2010 2009 2008 2007 2006 2005

Typeset by Fakenham Photosetting Ltd, Fakenham, Norfolk.
Printed in Italy for Hodder Arnold, an imprint of Hodder Education, a member of the Hodder Headline Group, 338 Euston Road, London NW1 3BH.

CONTENTS

Acknowledgements ii

Introduction v

Section 1. Enterprise 1

1.	Starting a business	2
2.	Business planning	4
3.	Business aims and objectives	6
4.	Stakeholders	8

Section 2. Organisation and growth 11

5.	Business organisation	12
6.	The administration function	14
7.	Business size	16
8.	Business growth	18

Section 3. Management and communication 21

9.	Management and leadership styles	22
10.	Motivating workers	24
11.	Managing change and decision-making	26
12.	Internal communication	28
13.	External communication	30
14.	IT support	32

Section 4. Business types 35

15.	Sole trader	36
16.	Partnerships	38
17.	Limited liability companies	40
18.	Franchises	42
19.	Multinationals and holding companies	44
20.	The public sector	46
21.	Cooperatives, charities and voluntary groups	48

Section 5. Finance and accounts 51

22.	The finance function	52
23.	Raising finance	54
24.	Costs and revenue	56
25.	Break-even	58
26/27.	Financial documents	60

28.	Cash flow forecasts and budgets	64
29.	Business accounts – the balance sheet	66
30.	Business accounts – the profit and loss account	68
31.	Understanding ratios	70
32.	Improving profitability	72

Section 6. Human resources   75

33.	Human resources function	76
34.	Pay and benefits	78
35.	Recruitment, training and retention	80
36.	Applying for a job	82
37.	Rights and responsibilities at work	84
38.	Industrial relations	86

Section 7. Production   89

39.	The chain of production	90
40.	The operations function	92
41.	Manufacturing methods	94
42.	Location of industry	96
43.	Producing efficiently	98
44.	Managing quality	100

Section 8. Marketing and sales   103

45.	The marketing and sales function	104
46.	Market planning and customer profiles	106
47.	Market research	108
48.	Customer service	110
49.	Measuring customer satisfaction	112
50.	Consumer protection	114

Section 9. The marketing mix   117

51.	Product	118
52.	Product life cycles	120
53.	Price	122
54.	Promotion	124
55.	Branding and image	126
56.	Distribution (place)	128

Section 10. External influences on business   131

57.	Business morals and ethics	132
58.	Business and government	134
59.	Business and the European Union	136
60.	Overseas trade	138

Succeeding   141

61.	Preparing for the exam	142
62.	Exam paper features	144
63.	Coursework: Single Award GCSE	146
64.	Coursework: Double Award Applied GCSE	148

Introduction

Rationale

Business Studies is increasingly popular in schools. It is seen as a subject that can help pupils on to either higher education or into a job. It has expanded into Applied Business Studies and awards such as BTEC. In many cases you will find yourself teaching the full range of students, from the highest ability to the lowest, often in the same class. This means that materials have to be differentiated to ensure that all pupils are receiving an equal chance of succeeding at their own level. Textbooks tend to cater for the top end of ability and in many cases are only usable with competent readers. In this text the language levels have been deliberately kept low. This means shorter sentences, simpler sentence construction and fewer multi-syllabic words. Of course, one of the problems with Business Studies is its use of technical language. Often pupils know and understand concepts – because of their own real life experience – but fail, in coursework and examinations, to use the technical words associated with them. The technical language is here, therefore, but presented in more user- friendly constructs. The rationale behind this text is thus that it is easier to make things more complex or detailed for higher ability pupils than to simplify them.

Structure

The text is structured in short Units, usually of just two pages, each of which provides an introduction, overview and examples for the concept being discussed. The Units are divided into sections, each of which starts with a full page diagram that can be used as the basis for a lesson or for revision. In the Unit itself, the 'Review' section reminds pupils of what they have learned and then moves them forward in a familiar context. The 'Read This' feature roots the concept in a real world example, where possible linked to current business news. One of the strengths of Business Studies as a subject is to trade on this relevance to issues that affect ordinary people. The Basics explains the minimum knowledge required for an understanding of the concept or issue. Short features then provide activities and exercises for visual, kinaesthetic and aural learners, and a reminder of the key terms used in the Unit.

Teacher's Resource

The Teacher's Resource contains details of the readability levels for each Unit along with further information and ideas on teaching. At the start of each section, there is information on how the topic relates to double and single GCSE with information on how the concept is tested. There are further exercises for pupils which include:

○ 'Do this Later' for homework and extended projects

○ 'Click on this' for ICT based work

○ 'Write this' for longer written exercises

There are also quick quizzes and games along with diagrams and material that can be projected on to interactive whiteboards. Comments and answers, where appropriate, for both the pupil book exercises and teacher resource ones are provided.

The resource also contains worksheets that can be downloaded and manipulated to your own requirements along with a full glossary of key terms.

TO THE STUDENT – HOW TO USE THIS BOOK

Welcome to the wonderful (and real) world of Business Studies. *Business Studies: The Essentials* guides you through all the core knowledge you will need to succeed in your chosen course. The book is split up into Sections and Units.

○ Each **Section** is a collection of Units about similar topics. At the start of each Section there is a full page diagram to get you started thinking about the topics in the Section. You can also come back to this and use it for revision. You can also use it as the basis for poster and display work.

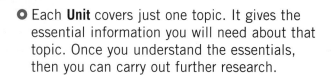

- Each **Unit** covers just one topic. It gives the essential information you will need about that topic. Once you understand the essentials, then you can carry out further research.

In each Unit you will see the following features:

REVIEW THIS

If this is the first Unit in a Section, this will introduce you to it. For later Units, this section reminds you of what you have learned, so that you can move on.

READ THIS

This is usually a real business issue, giving examples from the real world that help to explain the topic. Often they are news stories. Reading these will give you a good idea of why you need to learn about this topic.

THE BASICS

Read this to learn the essential knowledge about the topic. It will explain any difficult terms involved and show you how technical business words are used. If you understand THE BASICS then you are well on your way to succeeding in your course!

LOOK AT THIS

This is usually a photograph, diagram or cartoon to get you thinking about how and why the topic is important to business. It might also ask you to practice a skill or to show that you have understood about the topic.

DO THIS

This is an exercise for you to try. You may be asked to create something, or make something, or carry out something (like a survey, perhaps). Usually these are carried out with a partner or in a group, so that you can help each other. Sometimes you have to write a short report to say why you have done, or found out. This will help you to show that you understand the topic.

REMEMBER THIS

This is an even shorter version of the essential information about a topic! It cuts it down to just a few words, which you can use to check your understanding. You could try doing your own version of a REMEMBER THIS before reading this one, just to see how well you have learned the topic.

WORD BANK

Business Studies has a lot of technical terms. I bet that you know why a supermarket charges a really low price for an item that it puts in the far corner of the store, but I bet you didn't know it was called a 'loss leader'. The word bank helps you by defining the technical terms that you will need to use to earn top marks.

The last Section is there to help you when you start on coursework or have to revise for an examination. The advice is on:

- **Preparing for the exam** – this will help you with all the things you should do before an examination – like revising, staying calm and making sure you have the right equipment.

- **Exam paper features** – this will help you to understand the most common ways in which examination papers are set out, and help you on ideas such as what key words and marks per question mean.

- **GCSE Coursework** – this will help those of you who are doing coursework for a Single Award GCSE. It explains what you will need to do, how you can make this easier, and how to do well.

- **Applied GCSE Coursework** – this will help those of you who are doing coursework for a Double Award Applied GCSE. It explains what you will need to do, how you can make this easier, and how to do well.

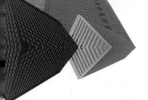

Enterprise

Unit 1 Starting a business

REVIEW THIS

People who start their own business are usually called **entrepreneurs**. There are many reasons for starting a business, although there is a risk of failure. As running a business is risky, a business prepares a business plan, which includes the business aims and targets. These aims and targets change once a business starts to grow. The larger the business, the more people and groups will have an interest in its success. People who invest in a business or are interested in it are called **stakeholders**.

READ THIS

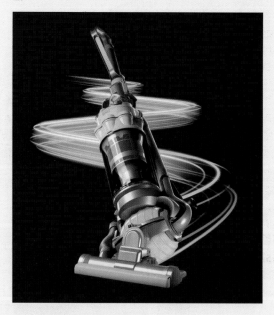

James Dyson – the entrepreneur
For over a hundred years, the vacuum cleaner used in our homes remained largely unchanged. The electric motor created a vacuum that sucked up dust and blew it into a bag. This bag was then either emptied or thrown away and replaced. One firm, Hoover, was so successful that it became the market leader. This resulted in people using its brand name for the product to describe their cleaning – hoovering.

Continued ➜

Then along came a man with a new idea – the bagless vacuum cleaner. James Dyson took several years to perfect his idea and he made sure that no one could copy his invention. Dyson tried to sell his idea to existing companies but no one was interested. Finally, he set up his own company, and with the help of some investors, launched the Dyson cleaner on to the market.

James Dyson is a good example of an entrepreneur. He came up with an idea. He improved on the product and risked much of his own money in the venture. When his cleaner proved successful, Dyson was able to expand the business and, with the help of others, Dyson plc has grown into a large and successful company.

THE BASICS

Why do people start their own business?
For some people there may be only one reason for starting a business, but for others there may be a mixture of reasons. For example:

- **you have lost your job and have received some redundancy money**
- **you want to be the boss and not have to work for someone else**
- **you have lots of skills and experience that you could use better**
- **you have a good idea**
- **you want a challenge in your life**
- **you want to make a reasonable living**
- **you want to make a large profit**.

Why do many businesses fail?
Most businesses start small and in many cases remain small. Only a few will grow to become large companies. Figures also show that a large number

of new start-up businesses fail within two years. Advisers have found that some of the main reasons for business failure are:

- **expecting sales and income to be larger than they are**
- **forgetting to calculate some costs**
- **failing to keep costs under control**
- **not having enough cash to pay debts**
- **charging the wrong price**
- **not changing the product to meet what the customer wants**
- **taking too many risks**
- **lacking enough money to help the business to grow**
- **not having enough skills and experience.**

Every day, while some businesses are succeeding, others are closing down. It is important therefore for new businesses to be set up so that jobs are created and people can continue to earn wages to buy goods and services.

 DO THIS

1 Look again at the reasons why people start a business. Try to think of some other reasons why someone might start up their own business. Plan a bubble chart or spider diagram to show all of the possible reasons. In the middle put the phrase, 'Possible reasons for starting a business'. In the bubbles, or on the spider legs, write in the key words for each reason.

Continued →

2 Look again at the reasons for a business failing. With a friend, try to think of five more possible reasons. Share your ideas with the rest of the class. Finally, draw up another bubble chart or spider diagram showing all the possible reasons for business failure.

LOOK AT THIS

Look again at the picture of Dyson's latest bagless vacuum cleaners. Remembering what you read earlier about James Dyson the entrepreneur, make a list of the possible reasons why you think his idea was so successful.

A-Z

WORD BANK

Entrepreneurs – people who think of a business idea, obtain some money to put their idea into action, organise and manage the business, hope to make a profit but risk making a loss and losing everything

Stakeholders – anyone with an interest in the success of a business

Redundancy money – a sum of money paid to people when they lose their job

Profit – this is the difference between the income a business earns from selling its goods and services, and all of the costs of making or providing them

Risks – for business people this means the possibility of losing all of the money they have put into the business if it fails

 REMEMBER THIS

Many hundreds of new businesses are started each year. Successful business people are called entrepreneurs as they show lots of enterprise in organising resources, risking their money and hoping to make a profit. Successful businesses create jobs and incomes for people.

Enterprise

Unit 2 Business planning

REVIEW THIS

At the heart of both business success and failure is money. Owners of a new business need to invest hundreds if not thousands of pounds to start it. They will also need money to keep the business running through its difficult early months. Few people will have enough money to pay for all the start-up and early running costs. Most businesses will need loans from a bank to get started. All banks will want to be sure that the loan will be paid back. To help decide whether to lend any money, a bank will want to see a business plan.

 READ THIS

Preparing a business plan will help a firm to obtain loans and other help from a bank. It will also be useful in other ways. First, it might be used to attract other people to put money into the business and to become joint owners. Second, remember the document is a plan so it will help the owners to think through all the details so that nothing is forgotten. Many business people will use the plan to help run the business. A checklist of ideas or key dates could be included. It could also spell out the roles of each person in the business. Finally, the plan might include some targets to help measure success. The owners could compare the business's actual performance with the targets to see if it is being successful.

THE BASICS

There are seven main sections that all plans should include. These are shown below (the order may vary a little in each case).

1 *Basic details:* the name and address of the business, key telephone numbers, the type of ownership, the type of product or service being sold and the target start date will all be included in the first part.

2 *Aims and objectives:* an overall aim for the business needs to be shown, followed by more specific objectives or targets. These will need to show what the business hopes to achieve in the first six months and by the end of the first and second years. You will also have to describe your market: who will buy and how many customers you expect.

3 *The product/service:* you will need to compare your product with two competitors on such things as price, appearance, quality and features.

4 *Pricing:* you will need a list of all costs and a calculation of break-even (see Unit 25).

5 *Promotion:* details of advertising and all other forms of promotion need to be given, along with their costs.

6 *Staff:* personal details of the owners need to be given, with details of the type of staff that need to be employed.

7 *Financial matters:* a list of all equipment and buildings, estimates of income and profits, and details of how much money is being put in by the owners and how much will need to be borrowed.

 DO THIS

Create your own business plan forms. You can do this by using the seven sections described above. Set out the parts of each section with space for a business person to fill in the details. This is best done using a word-processing package on a computer.

1. Does the product/service really work?

2. How does the product/service compare with those already on sale?

3. Do the owners and managers have enough skills and experience?

4. Are people really going to buy the product?

5. Are all the cost and income figures in the plan realistic?

6. Are the advertising and promotion plans good enough?

7. Has anything been missed out?

This mini-guide shows the key things that a bank has to consider when deciding whether to give a business a loan. Can you think of any other things you would want to consider?

WORD BANK

Income – the money earned from selling goods and services plus any other money gained from its operations.

Bank lending – loans offered to businesses by banks plus any other credit arrangements such as overdrafts.

REMEMBER THIS

Banks help people to start up and expand businesses by lending money and providing other services. Any bank lending money needs to be sure that the business will be able to afford the interest payments and to pay back the loan. To help judge this the bank will insist on a business plan before any money is lent. This plan will also help the business to organise and run its activities.

Unit 3 Business aims and objectives

REVIEW THIS

In Unit 2 you will have noticed that a business plan should include a section labelled 'aims and objectives'. Any business needs an overall aim but it will also need some more specific objectives. These will be targets that can be measured to see if the business is succeeding. Many targets will be linked to a period of time and will be changed when they have been achieved.

READ THIS

Many team sports have aims and objectives. This is particularly the case in professional football. Some of the top teams playing in the Coca-Cola Championship League will be aiming to gain promotion to the Barclays Premier League. Those at the bottom of the Premier League will have a very simple objective – to avoid relegation! A team at the top end of the Premier League will have several objectives. One will be to go on and win the league. Another is almost certainly to be highly successful in the European Champions League. The club might also have a long-term aim – to win at least one trophy each year.

THE BASICS

Aims are usually set for the business as a whole. For large businesses, these might be to be the 'world leader' or to 'provide products of the highest quality'. These aims might not be achieved for a long time and could be difficult to measure.

Some businesses call their aims 'mission statements' or even 'vision statements'. These are often a combination of aims and objectives. For example, at out-of-town factory outlet centres such as Royal Quays near Newcastle, most of the outlets have a board stating a broad aim and some of their objectives. These are intended both to inform and reassure customers about the special prices being charged on many of the product lines.

Objectives or targets are more specific and might be linked to just a part of a business. Objectives can be grouped together under three headings.

1 **Maximising objectives**, meaning the business is trying to make the most of something. Good examples include:

   (a) maximising profit – making the most profit possible

   (b) maximising sales – selling as many items as possible

   (c) maximising **turnover** – earning as much revenue as possible from selling a good or service.

2 **Trying to achieve a minimum** (which is an easier objective). Good examples include:

   (a) maintaining **market share** – keeping the firm's existing percentage of market share

   (b) earning a reasonable income – earning enough revenue or profit to keep the owners happy.

3 A wider range of objectives, including:

   (a) survival – to continue operating and perhaps break even

   (b) independence – to be self-employed and not having to work for someone else

   (c) growth – to expand the business by selling a wider range of products or by operating more outlets

   (d) reputation – to have a good name for quality and excellence.

All of these objectives are given to show you some typical examples. There may be lots of other examples that are equally valid. You also need to remember that most businesses will have more than one objective, and some may have several. The objectives will also vary with the type and size of business, and with how long it has been operating.

One way of judging objectives is to use the phrase SMART. Objectives ought to be:

S = specific and clearly worded
M = measurable so that the business can clearly see if they have been achieved
A = achievable, so that the business has a chance of reaching its target
R = realistic and relevant to that particular business
T = time-related – a deadline is set for achieving the objective.

DO THIS

In your class make a list of all the businesses in your local area. From the list select a range of ten different businesses. Try to select some small, some medium and some large ones. Try to include one that is quite new and another that has been operating for a long time. If possible, choose businesses that offer different types of goods and services to each other.

1 Create a three-column table. In the first column, write the name of each business you have selected. In the second column, write the long-term aims of the business. In the third column, write the objectives or targets of the business.

2 Try to find out, or guess, the likely aims and objectives of each of your chosen businesses, and write them in your table.

3 Share your ideas with the rest of the class. See if you notice any similarities and differences with their ideas.

WORD BANK

Turnover – the income or revenue earned from selling goods before any costs are paid

Market share – the portion of the total sales of a product gained by one business, usually given as a percentage figure

REMEMBER THIS

Aims and objectives are things that a business wants to achieve. If they are achieved, it means the business is probably succeeding. Each individual business has its own set of aims and objectives. These will vary according to the type, size, age and nature of the business.

Unit 4 Stakeholders

REVIEW THIS

In Unit 1 you learned how entrepreneurs put a lot of their own money into starting businesses. They obviously have the major stake in a business. In Unit 2 you learned that business plans can be used to attract extra finance from banks and other investors. They will also have an interest in the success of the business. The description of aims and objectives in Unit 3 showed that there are other groups who have an interest or hold a stake in the business. These are called stakeholders.

READ THIS

In Unit 3 you read about the aims and objectives of professional football teams. Lots of different groups also have a stake in the clubs. Three of the most obvious stakeholders will be the owners, the employees and the customers. The owners will be interested in making profit, or at least in running a successful club. The footballers are the clubs' employees, along with all the backroom staff, whose main interest may be the size of their wage packet. The customers will be the club supporters, who will want to be entertained and, hopefully, linked to a successful club. Other groups of stakeholders will include kit suppliers, sponsors and the manager.

DO THIS

1 Create a two-column table. Head the first column, 'Stakeholder group' and the second column 'Stake or interest'.

2 In the first column, list as many stakeholders in a football club as you can think of.

3 In the second column, describe the stake or interest each stakeholder will have in the football club.

THE BASICS

If you have an interest in something, then you have a stake in it. This makes you a stakeholder. Some stakeholders are part of the business and are known as **internal stakeholders**. These are the owners, managers and other employees. **External stakeholders** are customers, suppliers, creditors, competitors and the local community. They are not part of the business.

○ **Owners put a lot of money into the business. They hope that this money is safe and will earn them a profit. They are certainly interested in the success of their business.**

○ **Employees want a fair day's pay for a fair day's work. They need to know that their job is safe, and many will hope to gain promotion.**

○ **Managers share many aims with both owners and shareholders. They hope that the business is successful as it might help them to become an even bigger company. They will also hope to share in the profits as well as earning their salaries.**

○ **Customers expect value for money when they buy goods and services. They expect quality products that work and are at affordable prices.**

○ **Suppliers provide goods and services to a business. They require regular orders and need the business to pay for the supplies on time.**

- Creditors are people and companies who have lent money to a business. They will be very keen for the business to be able to afford to repay the money – with interest.

- Competitors are keen to know what and how a business is doing. They need to find out if new products are being launched, if prices are being changed and if new adverts are being used.

- The whole community is interested in the success of a business, which is providing jobs and services and may even attract other businesses to the area.

LOOK AT THIS

This picture shows a typical holiday hotel. Use this picture to create a mind map of the possible stakeholders in the hotel. For each stakeholder try to think what interest they will have in the hotel. Colour the internal stakeholders (staff?) in red and the external stakeholders (guests?) in blue.

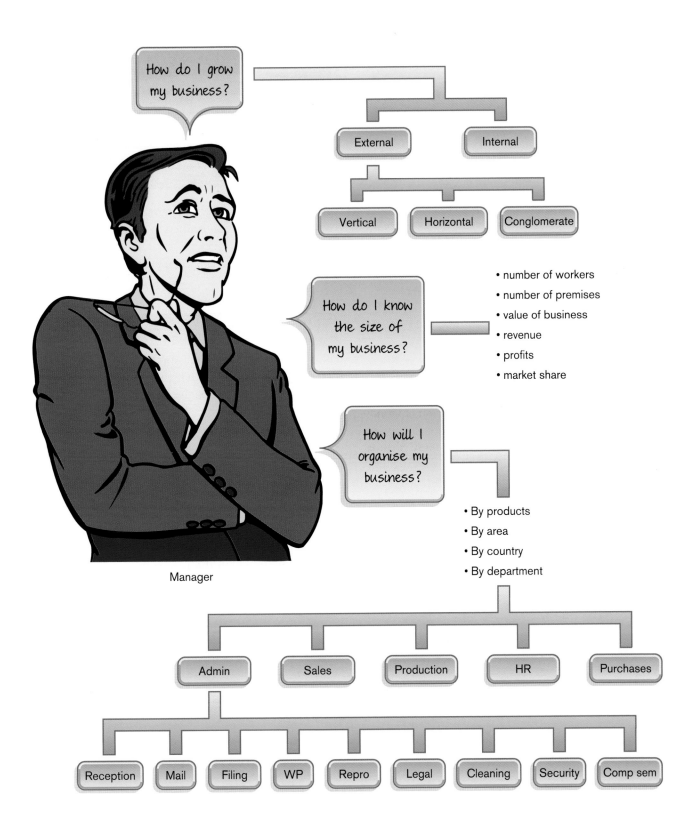

Unit 5 Business organisation

REVIEW THIS

In Section 1, you were introduced to the key groups of people who are involved in starting businesses. You also found out about the aims and objectives of business organisations and how they plan start-ups and expansions. In this section, you will first find out how a business is organised. This is followed up by finding out how important the administration department is to all firms. The final two units will show you how business size is measured and how businesses achieve growth.

READ THIS

Imagine working for a business that is not organised. How would you know what you had to? Who would be buying in the stock? Who would be in charge of different tasks? Who would make sure that you were paid for your effort? Even small businesses need to be organised so that everyone knows what they have to do. For large businesses, organisation is vital.

This is certainly the case for the Singapore Airlines Group. It has over 29,000 employees working for several subsidiary companies in over 80 locations around the world. The Group has tried to keep its organisation charts as flat as possible. This has helped it to give power to local managers to make

Continued →

the best decisions for customers. The Singapore Airlines Group is determined to keep a structure that helps its managers and staff to respond quickly in an ever-changing market.

THE BASICS

All businesses create some sort of **organisational structure**. This means that they divide up the main roles or tasks. Separate departments then carry out these functions. The departments need to be linked together in some way. They will need to work and communicate with each other.

The relationship between the departments and the overall organisational structure can be shown in an organisational chart like the one below. This is the best-known way to organise a business. Other ways include drawing the chart on a product basis or by the markets to which the firm sells.

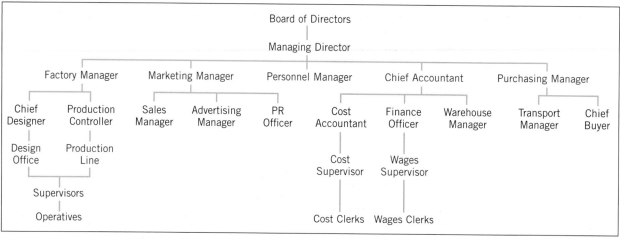

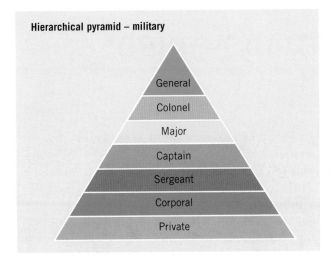

Hierarchical pyramid – military

General
Colonel
Major
Captain
Sergeant
Corporal
Private

Some people describe these organisation charts as a pyramid. This is because there are few people at the top, with the largest number of people working at the bottom of the organisation. This is shown in the diagram of a typical pyramid structure, above.

You can also see that there are several layers or levels in the organisation. Another way to describe this pyramid structure is a hierarchical organisation. This shows that a few people have the most **authority** at the top of the organisation. Those at the bottom have the least say in running the business.

The way in which power is passed down through the organisation is called the chain of command. If you look again at the pyramid diagram, you will see how decisions are passed down through the layers. If there are lots of layers, then passing decisions down can take a long time and it can be a complicated process. Workers at each level will be supervised by someone above them.

The **span of control** measures the number of workers directly controlled by one person. A narrow span of control might be between two and six people; a wide span of control will be at least seven people. The actual width of the span will depend on such things as the nature of the work, how much supervision is needed and the skills required.

The Board of Directors takes the major decisions in a business. It then passes on the responsibility for the day-to-day running of the company to the manager. This is known as **delegation**. The manager needs to be given the authority to make these decisions. Such authority is usually written up in a person's job description.

Some businesses try to improve their organisation by taking out one or more layers. This is known as **delayering**. This can speed up the decision-making process but can put more pressure on staff.

DO THIS

Schools are good examples of organisations that have a departmental structure.

1 Find out and make a list of all the subject departments in your school.

2 Find out and list the names of all the teachers in each department. Note the name of the teacher in charge of each department.

3 Note down the name of your headteacher and the names of all the other teachers on the senior leadership/management team.

4 Draw up an organisational chart for your school showing the structure of the departments and including the names of all the teachers. Put all the teachers in the right place and at the right level.

5 Discuss with your business studies teacher whether the organisational chart could be shown in some other way.

WORD BANK

Organisational structure – the way in which organisations are laid out

Authority – the power to make certain decisions

Span of control – the number of workers controlled by one person

Delegation – the passing down of authority to make decisions

Delayering – taking out one or more levels of management

REMEMBER THIS

All businesses need to be organised. The best structures help a business to meet its objectives. There are many ways to structure the business. Many businesses do this by departments. The largest businesses will have several layers. Some firms have tried to flatten their structure by taking out one or more layers.

Unit 6 The administration function

REVIEW THIS

Most businesses organise themselves by departments. Arguably one of the most important departments is the administration department. Its work is to help all the other departments operate properly. Much of its work seems quite simple but, without it, the business could grind to a halt.

 READ THIS

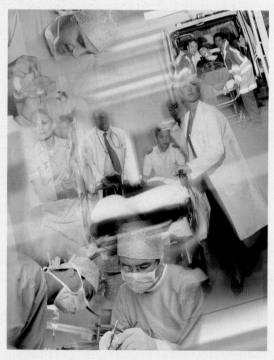

Some of the biggest administration departments can be found in organisations within the public sector. Government departments, local councils and hospitals depend heavily on people working in administration. Look at this picture of a major hospital. The main work of the hospital is to help the sick and injured, with doctors and nurses at the heart of this healthcare. But nothing would work well without a huge army of people providing administrative services. Step in the door and you would see reception dealing with visitors and taking phone calls. Walk down the corridor to a ward, and you will find a secretary

Continued →

making appointments and dealing with both written and computer records. Some of the staff you see will be cleaners making regular rounds of the whole building. Staff and patient meals will have to be provided, while the whole building will also require regular maintenance and security.

THE BASICS

The main role of this department is to provide all the service operations required by an organisation. How it is organised will depend on the type and size of the firm. Typical operations by the administrative department include the following.

1 *Reception:* this deals with all visitors to the firm. It represents the first impression that visitors gain of the firm. Usually it also deals with incoming phone calls.

2 *Mail handling:* incoming mail needs to be sorted and delivered to the right departments. Some firms open mail centrally, before delivering it to the appropriate section. Outgoing mail is collected and sent out using either the post office or private courier firms. In the largest organisations, mail might have to be moved between different departments.

3 *Filing/clerical/word processing/data processing:* in most firms a multi-skilled worker is needed to handle these sorts of jobs. While many firms increasingly keep records on computer, most still have paper records that need to be filed. A good example here will be GPs. These doctors use computers to maintain records, but also have large paper records as back-up.

4 *Reprographics:* in some firms there is a need to print multiple copies of written materials. In some organisations it may be cheaper to have a central reprographics section rather than a photocopier in each office. Just think how much printing the exam boards need to do.

5 *Legal services:* all companies must, by law, have someone to act as **Company Secretary**. This person keeps a record of any meetings of the Board of Directors. He or she must make sure that the company acts legally, and is often in charge of the whole department. Other organisations, such as councils, have a large legal section because there are lots of laws that control the way they operate.

6 *Cleaning and maintenance:* manufacturers may have a specialised, separate **maintenance** section. Service providers, however, may have a small section to deal with minor day-to-day problems. It may also be responsible for cleaning the premises. A good example of this is the service provided by caretakers in schools.

7 *Security:* the need for security varies greatly between businesses. Those with large valuable premises and those producing valuable or dangerous materials will need continuous security – often involving 24-hour security personnel. Shops and many offices may be able to depend on a security alarm and the watchfulness of all staff.

8 *Computer services:* those businesses that depend on computers need specialist computer experts to maintain both the hardware and software. In most businesses, these will be a part of the administration department.

 DO THIS

Go back to the 'Read this' section and think about a hospital near you.

1 Make a list of as many administrative jobs you can think of that are linked to a hospital.

2 Carry out some research into the type of work involved in these jobs.

3 Create a poster to describe the work of ten of these jobs. Use suitable pictures or drawings. You might try to create this poster on a computer.

4 Use your poster to explain the work of your chosen workers to the rest of your class.

WORD BANK

Company Secretary – a director of a company, who keeps the company legally correct

Maintenance – a section of workers carrying out minor repairs and servicing work on buildings and equipment

 REMEMBER THIS

Few organisations are able to operate without a department to look after essential administration. The department provides key support to all the other departments. Typical tasks include reception and telephone duties, mail handling, cleaning and maintenance, clerical duties, legal advice, security and computer services. Some people suggest that administrative services are just as important to a business as oil is in the engine of a car.

Unit 7 Business size

REVIEW THIS

Many businesses want to expand. This unit gives you some of the reasons for businesses wanting to grow, and explains how we decide when a business may be classed as small, medium or large. You will also find out why so many businesses remain small.

 READ THIS

The Dixons Group plc is Europe's leading specialist electrical retailer. How do we know it is the biggest? First, it has five main retail brands: Dixons, Currys, PC World, PC World Business and The Link. Together these retailers have over 1,440 stores in 12 different countries. The company employs more than 30,000 people. Sales revenue for the company reached more than £5.8 billion in the financial year ending in March 2003. This helped it to achieve more than £301 million profit. However you measure it, Dixons Group plc has to be Europe's biggest specialist electrical retailer.

THE BASICS

There are many different ways of measuring the size of a business. Choosing the best method depends mainly on the type of goods or services being made and sold.

○ You could simply count the number of people who work for the business. Fewer than ten would suggest it was small. Up to 100 might make it a medium-sized business, so more than 100 would make it large. The only trouble is that some businesses do not need many workers, and yet would still be called large businesses.

○ Another simple way to measure the size of a business is to count the number of premises owned. A retailer with only one or two shops would be small while a retailer with 20 outlets would be large. The only problem with this measure is that a manufacturer might have only one or perhaps two very large factories. In some cases a business might be measured by the number of regions or even countries that it operates in. Some of the largest businesses in the world – such as McDonald's – operate in almost every country in the world.

○ This gives a clue to another way of measuring business size: the value of everything owned by the business could be added up. This would include all the buildings and land it owned, as well as all the equipment and vehicles. If the value came to less than £1 million, the business would be small; if the business was worth over £3 million it would be large.

○ Another useful way to measure business size is to calculate a firm's income or revenue from selling goods and services. **Sales revenue** of less than £2 million would put the business in the small category. Large firms would be classed as earning more than £8 million. You might think that you could use profits as a way of measuring business size. The problem with this is that **profit** depends on how successful a business is. Both small and large firms can be very profitable. Equally they can both be capable of earning only small profits, or even of making a loss.

○ One final way to measure business size is to calculate the firm's **market share**. This means working out a business's sales as a proportion of the total market. The firm with the largest percentage figure will be the biggest firm in that market.

A plumber with his van – working for a small firm

For many businesses, the best way for them to survive is to grow larger. Higher sales usually help to make a business more profitable. The larger the business, the easier it will be able to compete against other companies. A large business gains many advantages simply from being large. For example, it may be able to buy supplies in bulk and therefore buy them at a discount. It may be able to afford research into better products and production methods. Some businesses may want to grow so that they are the biggest firm and can dominate the market.

There are roughly four million small firms in the UK. The reasons for this include:

- **many businesses provide a local service – for example, a plumber**
- **many firms have only recently started up, and most start life with a single owner**
- **many businesses lack enough money to expand**
- **many businesses supply specialist products to a small market**
- **many owners want their business to remain small.**

Unit 8 Business growth

REVIEW THIS

Unit 7 looked at all the possible ways to measure the size of a business. It also suggested some of the reasons why so many firms remain small. This unit looks in detail at why some firms want to grow. It also explains how firms can achieve this growth and the direction they can take.

READ THIS

MFI is probably the UK's largest retailer of kitchens, bedrooms and appliances. It manufactures furniture, it operates as a retailer and it provides services to the customers who buy its products. MFI has achieved this through both internal and external growth. Internal growth has been achieved by developing and selling new products, both to keep existing customers happy and to attract new ones to its existing stores. It has continually modernised these stores in order to increase sales. External growth has been tried through a link-up with the Sofa Workshop Company.

THE BASICS

When a manufacturing firm grows, it might be adding factories or warehouses. A retailer might increase the number of its shops. Expansion might involve adding a wider range of products. Growth of a business might increase the number of workers. It might also involve introducing new technology.

Most growth is achieved internally by the business. This does not involve any outside business, and the firm finds resources to expand the business gradually. It might rent or buy another shop, or add a new range of products alongside its usual ones. For example, many garden centres have expanded at their existing site by adding a garden furniture section alongside the usual sales of plants. Many bakers' shops have introduced sales of sandwiches and drinks alongside the sale of bread, cakes and pastries. Much of this growth will be funded by the business saving up its profits. It could also borrow money to expand in this way. The main problem with **internal growth** is that it tends to be quite slow.

The other type of growth is achieved externally. One way is for two businesses to join together. This is called a **merger**. For example, a lot of the high-street banks have been created by mergers; NatWest bank was created in the 1960s by a merger between the National Provincial and the Westminster banks. The other way is for one business to take over another. A well-known example of this is the **take-over** of Asda by the American giant company Wal-Mart.

A big advantage of external growth is that the newly created business will immediately be bigger. The major problem is that there is no guarantee of success and not all merged firms manage to achieve their expected targets. There are three ways to achieve external growth.

1 **Horizontal integration**: this is when two firms producing the same goods at the same stage of production merge together. For example, Ford took over the car manufacturer Jaguar. The new company was immediately bigger and had more market power.

2 **Vertical integration**: this is when two firms merge together at different stages in the chain of production. One example might be a bread manufacturer merging with or taking over a company selling bread through its bakers' shops. This is called 'forwards' vertical integration because it moves towards the final

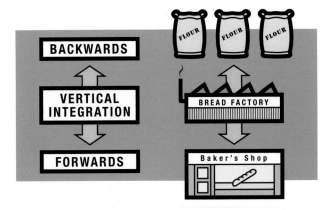

Internal growth – a business puts resources into new factories or shops

Mergers – two firms agreeing to join together to make a single larger business

Take-over – one firm takes control of another

Horizontal integration – merging with another business that makes the same type of good or service at the same stage of production

Vertical integration – merging with a business at an earlier or later stage in the chain of production

Conglomerate integration – merging with a business that produces a completely different type of good or service to your company

customer. If the bread manufacturer merged with a flour mill, the direction would be called 'backwards' vertical integration. Moving forwards along the chain of production helps to promote and sell products. Moving backwards helps to ensure supplies.

3 **Conglomerate integration**: this is when mergers or take-overs involve firms with no links between their products. For example, the bread manufacturer might merge with the car manufacturer. This sounds quite unlikely, but many large firms sell unrelated products. The main reasons for growing in this direction are to spread risks and to find more profitable markets. Another name for this is 'product diversification'.

REMEMBER THIS

While many firms are happy to stay the same size, there are many others looking to expand their businesses. Some do this by expanding internally, gradually putting more money into new products and new premises. Others expand externally through mergers and take-overs. Expansion can take various directions.

DO THIS

Re-read The Basics. Create a five-column table as shown below, and try to fill in as many details as possible.

Direction of growth	Description	Example	Advantages	Disadvantages
Vertical integration forwards				
Vertical integration backwards				
Horizontal integration				
Conglomerate integration				

LEADERSHIP STYLES

?

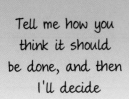

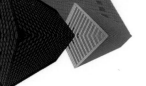

Unit 9 Management and leadership styles

REVIEW THIS

Unit 5 described the main departments found in an organisation. This unit looks at how such departments and how the whole business can be managed. In particular it looks at the way in which managers can use different styles to lead employees. An important part of leadership is to motivate workers so that they work hard. This may be done by using attractive pay schemes. Workers may also be motivated by perks and by being shown that they are valued. Leadership also means managing changes that have to take place within a business. Central to any change is communication. Both internal and external methods of communication will be used to help change take place. Communication will also help managers in their day-to-day running of the business.

READ THIS

When you next watch an interview with a major football club manager, think about his management and leadership skills. How does he manage his players? Does he plan every last move or does he ask the players their opinions and ideas? When it comes to motivating his players, does he shout at them when things go wrong or does he quietly talk things through? Think about everything that has to be done before a match takes place. What staff will be required and what skills will they need? How will they know what is expected of them?

THE BASICS

So what is management? Management involves setting targets, making decisions, giving responsibility to other people to carry out tasks, and motivating workers. This means that anybody who is a manager must have certain qualities. They need to be: responsible; trustworthy; motivated; decision-makers; leaders.

In large businesses there will be several layers, or levels, of management. In a manufacturing company the levels in the production department might look like this:

Managing Director
↓
Production Director
↓
Senior Production Manager
↓
Middle Production Manager
↓
Junior Production Manager
↓
Production Supervisor

This shows that managers have to communicate both upwards and downwards. The middle manager, for example, will be receiving information and instructions from the senior manager. These will be turned into action plans for the junior manager. Ideas and opinions will also be passed back up this **management chain**. Managers also have to communicate with the other managers operating at the same level.

How does management take place?

Management is about making decisions. This is often shown as a circular process because it is continuous. One version of this is the **management cycle** shown below.

The starting point in this cycle is usually when a director sets a target for managers to achieve. The managers will then create a plan. This plan is then communicated to all the departments and all the workers who need to be involved. The plan needs to be put into action, with managers organising all the necessary work. Managers will need to make sure that each worker and each department carries out their tasks at the right time and in the right order. This requires **coordination**.

The managers will also need to check that the work is carried out correctly. In other words, managers will monitor the workers and their efforts. Once the target is reached, managers will review how well the plan has worked, and then decide what new targets to set.

What is leadership?

Leadership is one key role for management. This does not really show up in the management cycle diagram. Managers can use several different leadership styles or techniques. The key styles are described below.

- ● **Autocratic:** this type of leader makes most of the decisions without anyone else being involved. The leader is very much the boss, and everyone is expected to do as they are told. Decisions are likely to be very clear, but employees do not really feel involved in the company.

- ● **Democratic:** this is different to autocratic since all managers are involved in decision-making and may be asked to vote on key matters. This helps to motivate workers, but it can take a long time to make the decisions.

- ● **Laissez-faire:** this is the complete opposite to autocratic, as managers are left to carry out their roles in their own ways. General guidelines and targets are laid down but managers are left to achieve the targets in their own way. This is highly motivating but some managers may not be clear as to what they have to do.

An example of autocratic leadership

Unit 10 Motivating workers

REVIEW THIS

We all like to feel valued, and we like to be rewarded when we succeed. At school, being praised or receiving certificates and prizes make us feel good. Most students will try to work even harder as a result. When we start work, employers often use a number of ways to persuade us to work hard. Pay and rewards, bonuses and perks, praise and promotion can all motivate us. The benefits for the business are more goods being made and a higher quality of service.

 READ THIS

Taylor Woodrow plc is a worldwide business, but in the UK its main business activity is housebuilding. This is mainly done through its Bryant brand. The company first motivates its workers through good pay. Bonuses are then available to all individuals, linked to good performance by the whole business. For some key workers, perks and other incentives are also given to retain their services. The company links all of these rewards to a review of each worker's performance.

THE BASICS

Motivation is the way in which workers can be encouraged to do a good job and to work harder. It also means finding ways to persuade workers to produce high-quality goods and services. Some ways of motivating workers will use money to encourage them. There are also other ways not linked to money. Before we decide how to motivate workers, we need to understand why people want to work.

Why do we work?

The main reason people work is to earn money to buy essential items. These include food, shelter and clothing. Once people have obtained the essentials, they need money to buy all the other items they want. This will help people to improve their **standard of living** and so have a better life.

There are also other reasons why people work. Most of us want to use the knowledge and skills that we have. Work helps to keep us active and gives us a satisfaction from carrying out our jobs. In many cases we work with groups of people. This helps us to satisfy our need to meet and interact with people. Finally, many people find their jobs give them a certain **status**. This means the job makes them feel valued and appreciated.

How do we motivate?

Now that we know why people work, we can sort out ways to motivate workers. The use of pay is one major way to motivate workers. If people need money to pay both for their essential needs and for all of their other wants, businesses can use special types of pay scheme to motivate workers. These are usually used with workers who are paid wages. This means they are normally paid at an hourly rate. Some pay schemes used on top of this time rate include the following.

● *Piece rate:* this means paying workers for the amount they produce. The more workers make, the more they are paid. This encourages workers to work faster and to produce more goods that the company can then sell. One problem that may result is if workers rush their work and quality falls.

● *Overtime rate:* this is paid when a job cannot be finished in the time allowed for it. This helps the firm because the job will be completed. It also helps the worker because the rate of pay will be increased. For example, overtime is often paid at 'time and a half' or even 'double time'. Disadvantages are the increase in the firm's costs, and the workers perhaps becoming very tired from working long hours.

○ *Bonus payments:* **these are extra payments often paid to encourage people to complete a job on time. They can also be used as a reward for high quality. They are used particularly to reward teams of workers.**

Many workers are paid an annual salary. This is then divided into 12 monthly payments. Such workers are less likely to be paid piece rates. Instead, they may receive perks or `fringe benefits`. One of the most best-known perks is the use of a company car, but this is not available to a large number of employees. Other perks include health insurance schemes, subsidised travel and store discounts.

Another method of motivation includes the use of incentives. These are mainly used for people working in sales. A commission pay scheme is used to encourage sales people by paying them a percentage of any sales revenue they earn for the company. Bonuses, prizes and even trophies can be used to persuade workers to put in extra effort.

Finally, there is a method of motivation linked to the idea of appreciation. Employers often find ways to show their workers that they care – that they are appreciated. This means involving workers in the decision-making process and helping their overall development.

DO THIS

Your family is likely to include a number of people who have worked for several years.

1 In a small group, make a list of questions to ask your families about:
  (a) which things motivate them
  (b) which things motivate them the most
  (c) which motivation methods are used by their places of work
  (d) which methods they think are best, and why.

2 Put the questions in the best order, and word-process the final question sheet.

3 Carry out the survey as part of your homework.

4 In your groups, share your results. Discuss what you have found out.

5 Write a short report with the main features of your findings.

WORD BANK

Standard of living – people's ability to buy the goods and services they desire

Status – a person's feeling of importance, usually linked to the type of job and their importance to the business

Fringe benefits – benefits received by an employee in addition to their wage or salary

REMEMBER THIS

Businesses want their employees to work hard and well. To do this they use pay, rewards and other methods to motivate them. The best motivation methods are linked to the things people want from their work.

Unit 11 Managing change and decision-making

REVIEW THIS

Businesses and the business world are constantly changing. Change might take place within the business, but much will take place outside. Some changes will be expected but there will always be some that come as a complete surprise. Whatever the change, businesses have to make many hundreds of decisions every day. Some are simple, everyday decisions, while others will have an impact much later on. The most effective businesses will try to manage this change by using a step-by-step process.

READ THIS

In 2004, Marks & Spencer plc once more found itself in a position of falling sales and profits. Senior management faced a number of decisions. Some were the everyday decisions of how much stock to buy in and how to promote the company's products. They also had to review many of their tactical decisions. These included what new food lines to order in and which new fashion designers to hire for the next two years. The most difficult and most important decisions were how to plan the future of the company. One key strategy decision saw the announcement in July 2004 of the closure of the company's Life Store. This was just a few months after it had first opened its doors at its Gateshead site, in February of that year.

THE BASICS

Every day, managers make many decisions. These decisions can be grouped under three headings.

1 **Operational decisions**: these decisions are made to keep the business running from day to day. Examples might include ordering new stock, deciding on special offers and advertising for new employees.

2 **Tactical decisions**: these decisions make changes to the way in which the business is run. They might involve changing product lines, changing transport methods, introducing new ways of making the product or deciding to increase the size of the workforce.

3 **Strategic decisions**: these involve making plans for the future and are taken by top management. Typical decisions might be to change the firm's targets, decide how to expand the business or even to consider a merger with another business.

You will have noticed that all of these decisions involve some sort of change. Changes are either internal or external, expected or unexpected.

- An internal change is one that the business can control. For a chocolate manufacturer, this might be the decision to introduce a new bar of chocolate.

- An external change is one that is outside the control of the business. This might be a change in customers' tastes for chocolate bars.

- Some changes are expected. For the chocolate manufacturer, this might be an advertising campaign by a competitor in response to the launch of its new chocolate bar.

- Many businesses will face lots of unexpected changes. An example for the chocolate manufacturer might be a sudden rise in the price of cocoa beans. This will push up the costs of making chocolate.

Managing change

There are four steps to managing change. Whether a change is expected or not, a business must first **plan for change**. It will need to identify where the company is now. It will need to decide targets to set for both costs and quality. The final part of the plan is to decide how to reach those targets.

The second step is **implementation** of the plan. This simply means the plan needs to be carried out. This can cause problems as some people do not like change. They might like things as they are and may be worried that their pay or job will be affected. To overcome this resistance, people need to be informed about the change. Best of all, they need to be actively involved in the change.

The third step in managing change is **control**. The business needs to make sure that change is carried out as set out in the plan. It also needs to make sure that any problems are dealt with in the best way. The business will often set targets for each stage of the change. If everyone knows what is expected of them, change is more likely to be successful.

The final step of managing change is **review**. Once the change is complete, managers will want to review the whole process to see if it has been completed successfully and if improvements could have been made. More importantly, they will want to decide what to do next.

Imagine you are the manager of a local branch of a supermarket near your school.

1 Make a list of all the decisions you might have to make in one day.

2 On a large piece of paper or card, create three columns with the headings 'Operational decisions', 'Tactical decisions' and 'Strategic decisions'. Use your list of decisions from the first part of this activity to put five examples of each type of decision in the right columns.

3 Your head office has told you that your branch is to introduce 24-hour opening in eight weeks' time. As a class, discuss how you, as the manager, could plan and manage this change.

REMEMBER THIS

Businesses are constantly changing. Sometimes the reason for change comes from within the business. Sometimes change is taking place outside and the business has to react to it. This means the business has a number of decisions to make: some for today but many for the future.

WORD BANK

Operational decisions – decisions made to keep the business running from day to day

Tactical decisions – decisions that will make changes to the way the business is run

Strategic decisions – decisions made by top management and that involve making major plans for the future

Plan for change – creating a plan that sets targets and shows how change will take place

Implementation – putting the planned change into operation

Control – making sure that the change takes place according to the plan

Review – checking that the planned change has taken place in the right way

Unit 12 Internal communication

REVIEW THIS

Good communication is vital to the effective running of a business. Communication basically consists of four parts: a sender and a receiver, the message itself and the medium. (The medium is the way in which the message is sent.) Businesses need to decide how best to communicate within the organisation. Sometimes communications will be informal. At other times, they need to be quite formal and linked to certain rules. Some communication methods are verbal, while others are written.

READ THIS

Think about your school. How does it communicate with you and your parents? Before you started at your school, your parents will have received a prospectus telling you all about the school. You probably paid a visit in the term before you actually started. Your teachers will have told you about rules and timetables, and you will have looked at a map of the school. Once there, you received messages from bulletins, during assemblies, by letter and through reports. You also gave messages back to your teachers and of course to your fellow students.

THE BASICS

Communication channels are the routes by which communications take place. Internal communication takes place within the business. Channels may be either formal or informal. **Formal channels** will be organised and will usually include a record of whatever has taken place. **Informal channels** can take place at any time and almost anywhere. They are often not organised and are unlikely to be recorded. Channels may be either written or oral.

Oral channels of communication

Oral channels involve the spoken word. Informal oral channels in a business are likely to include conversations, instructions, telephone calls, unplanned meetings and general gossip. A surprising amount of communication will take place in informal, unplanned talks, and very little will be formally recorded.

Formal oral channels are planned methods of communication and might include presentations, lectures and speeches. Conferences will almost certainly use these methods to inform people about the company, its products and its plans. Planned meetings will form a major part of formal, oral channels of communication. Most business meetings will have an agenda of points that need to be discussed.

Of course, meetings do not have to involve lots of people. A formal meeting may take place between

An example of video-conferencing

two people to discuss problems, to plan action or to review matters. The meetings do not even have to take place in the same room. New technology makes it possible for people to take part in video conferencing, even if they are in different parts of the world.

Written channels of communication

Informal written channels are likely to be some form of notes. They might be key points that somebody needs to remember from a phone call or from a meeting. The notes might be written up in a diagram. One example is a spider diagram (sometimes called a mind map). This often helps people to remember all the different parts of a long discussion or a complicated issue. Many people use 'post-its' as a quick, informal way to pass a written communication. Noticeboards are likely to display lots of informal written communications, such as reminders of nights out, or simple messages from fellow workers. Even a newsletter is quite informal in the way it passes on information to people.

Formal written communications will be at the heart of business. Meetings will have a written record of the main points and the action that needs to be taken. These records are called 'minutes'. All businesses need to hold documents as a formal record of their activities. There are four main varieties.

1 *Memoranda (memos)*. **These are short, written messages or reminders. They will be written on some sort of headed paper to make them official. As they are brief, only a few key points will be included.**

2 *Letters.* **These will be written on headed notepaper. They will act as a very formal record of actions. For example, a letter might be written warning an employee about his/her actions at the workplace.**

3 *Reports.* **These could be on a wide range of topics. The marketing department might report on the success of a recent advertising campaign, for example.**

4 *Documents.* **These will include pre-printed forms to record orders or to note down telephone conversations with customers. Large numbers of documents are needed for employees. Details of pay, pensions, holidays, training records and health and safety matters need to be recorded and kept.**

DO THIS

Your class plans to run a fundraising event in aid of a charity of your choosing. You need to tell the rest of the school about the event and persuade them to get involved.

1 Decide on a suitable event (real or imaginary).

2 Decide how you are going to tell the rest of the school about the event. Produce examples of any written communications, and plan out any verbal communications you are going to use.

3 Test the materials on another class to check that you are communicating the right message in the best way.

WORD BANK

Communication channels – the routes that communications and messages take from the sender to the receiver

Formal channels – channels of communication that have rules

Informal channels – channels of communication that do not have rules

REMEMBER THIS

It is important that an organisation chooses the correct channel of communication for each message. The channels may be formal or informal. Formal channels will have certain rules. Often formal channels must be used, but no business will operate without informal channels.

Unit 13 External communication

REVIEW THIS

Every day a company will receive hundreds, if not thousands, of communications from outside the business. A large number will be in written form, on paper, or in electronic form. An equally large number of inward communications will be in verbal form. Some of these communications will need a reply. Such replies will be a small part of the company's outward communications. The company's good reputation will be linked to how well it handles both inward and outward external communication.

 READ THIS

Inland Revenue

The Inland Revenue is responsible for collecting various taxes both from people and businesses. For example, it collects income tax, which is the government's biggest source of funding from tax. As this organisation delivers important services to the community, it needs clear and effective communications. Major **inward communications** include the tax forms that people and businesses fill in to tell the Inland Revenue about their income and expenditure. The organisation also receives hundreds of verbal enquiries each day from people seeking advice and wanting to report a change in their circumstances. Major **outward communications** include both verbal and written advice to people and business, as well as written statements of the amounts of tax that people and businesses have to pay.

THE BASICS

Businesses need to communicate with other businesses. This could be with suppliers, customers and government organisations. Any communication that takes place between the business and an outside body is called an external communication. The communications could be formal or informal, and could be written or oral.

Oral external communication

Informal oral channels include telephone calls, unplanned meetings and something called **networking**. Networking typically takes place when people start to talk during the coffee and lunch breaks at conferences or at social gatherings. Ideas and information can be shared and lots of new contacts can be made. Few records will be kept of these informal oral communications.

Formal oral channels can take many forms. Some telephone calls can be quite formal, particularly if a conference call is made with more than two people using telephones in loudspeaker mode. Many meetings with outside bodies and people are likely to be quite formal, with written records kept. Sometimes a business may send someone to a conference to give a presentation about the company.

Written external communication

Informal written communications with outside bodies used to be quite rare. Nowadays, this has all changed with the rapid expansion of email. Most emails tend to be short and to the point. They are often quite informal in the way they are written. If necessary, a record of the email can be kept, particularly if there is an attachment with it. One problem with emails is that there is no guarantee that the receiver actually reads them. Another problem is that emails are not secure.

From:	Liz Smith
Sent:	05 May 2005 14:31
To:	Tom Phillips
Subject:	Meeting

Please can we move the meeting forward to 3pm?

Much external communication is carried out using formal written documents. The main types of document include:

- O **letters of enquiry that ask for information or other items**
- O **catalogues or leaflets giving information about the company's products**
- O **order forms to buy goods from other businesses**
- O **invoices – requests for payments following the sale of goods and services**
- O **legal documents such as tax returns and company accounts and reports.**

These documents are needed for a number of reasons. The business needs to keep an official and formal record of transactions. Many of these need to use a standard layout for security reasons. With the increasing use of technology, a business tends to use pre-prepared documents that have to be used on specific machinery. A business is also likely to need lots of copies of some documents, so a standard format will be created.

DO THIS

Our daily post includes a huge amount of 'junk mail'. Over a period of two weeks, ask your parents if you can collect this mail and bring it into school. Create a display. In groups, discuss what messages the companies sending the mail are trying to communicate.

WORD BANK

Inward communications – communications being received from a sender outside the organisation

Outward communications – communications being sent to people and bodies outside the organisation

Networking – an informal way of communicating with other people or companies

REMEMBER THIS

It is important that an organisation chooses the right channel of communication for both incoming and outgoing messages. Channels may be formal or informal. Formal channels usually have a set of rules and are likely to involve forms and documents.

Unit 14 IT support

REVIEW THIS

Information and communications technology (ICT) has become increasingly important in all businesses. It can make communication faster, cheaper and more effective. The government has recognised its importance by making training and education in ICT a compulsory part of the subjects taught at school. Further training is actively encouraged and supported through colleges and other training providers. As developments in ICT continue to take place at a fast speed, more and more training will be needed.

READ THIS

More and more companies are looking for an **integrated information system**. This allows huge quantities of information to be handled. Such a system allows workers to be more accurate, and reduces costs for organisations. It also improves the services offered to customers. One such provider of integrated information systems is Canon. Originally founded in Japan, it is now a global company. It provides hardware and software that link together in a whole package. These packages are designed to meet the specific size and needs of each organisation. In many cases, an organisation can lease the packages rather than buy them outright.

THE BASICS

All departments within a business can benefit from the use of ICT through the use of both hardware and software. **Hardware** includes computers, screens, keyboards, printers and other items of equipment. **Software** refers to the programs used by the hardware. A business will be able to use a number of programs to help run its operations and to reduce costs. The main programs will include:

- **word processing** – documents can be created on screen, then edited with improvements to layout before final printing
- **databases** – lots of information can be stored in records, sorted and searched for
- **spreadsheets** – used to store numerical information, with calculations automatically carried out
- **desktop publishing** – this allows leaflets and presentations to be professionally produced
- **email** – sending messages from one computer to another
- **intranet** – web pages and email created within and only available to an organisation
- **internet** – the huge collection of web pages that can be accessed from most computers.

Benefits of using ICT

There are five main benefits to a business from using ICT.

1 Using ICT helps to speed up *communications*, both within a business and with external contacts. It also makes the whole process of communication far more efficient. Word-processing letters allows mistakes to be corrected before printing and, of course, they can be saved for future use. It is probably emailing that has changed communications the most. It has reduced the need for some phone calls. It is much quicker than depending on the post. With the development of intranets within organisations, internal communications have benefited greatly.

2 *Data storage and handling* used to be completely paper-based. This was expensive and clumsy, with a lot of time spent in filing information. Databases and spreadsheets have

helped businesses to move towards the paperless office. All sorts of records can be stored on a computer; for example, employee records, stock records, customer records and cash details. The real benefit comes when data can easily be found and used.

3 *Customer service* has gained much from the use of ICT. Customers who order through the internet are able to track the progress of their orders. This has also been used by Royal Mail so that customers can check where a parcel has got to. Email enquiries from customers allow customer services to respond quickly and in detail.

4 The use of ICT has helped many businesses improve their *security arrangements* in handling all forms of information. Systems can be created to protect confidential information. The use of log-in names and passwords are a core part of such security systems. In many organisations, there are separate departments that help to maintain the ICT systems, and protect the computer system from hacking and viruses.

5 Most shops now use *bar code scanners*. These are linked to a central computer. They allow the correct price to be charged, and are linked to the various ways to collect payment from the customer. Business costs are helped through linking the bar code to the storage of the stock. This can allow stock to be checked easily and re-ordered automatically.

DO THIS

Carry out a survey of computer/ICT usage in your school. Write a report of your findings that includes:

- the different types of hardware in use
- the different software packages in use
- the different uses of ICT by both staff and students.

WORD BANK

Integrated information systems – the linking of hardware and software through networks to manage all ICT tasks

Hardware – the actual machines used in ICT including computers, visual display units (VDUs) and printers

Software – the programs used by computers

REMEMBER THIS

ICT is so important that the government wants everyone to be well trained in its use. Internal ICT systems include networks and the intranet. Externally, the internet is the main system. The main types of software used are word-processing, spreadsheet and database programs. There are also a wide range of specialist programs for a business to use in carrying out its tasks, such as keeping accounts.

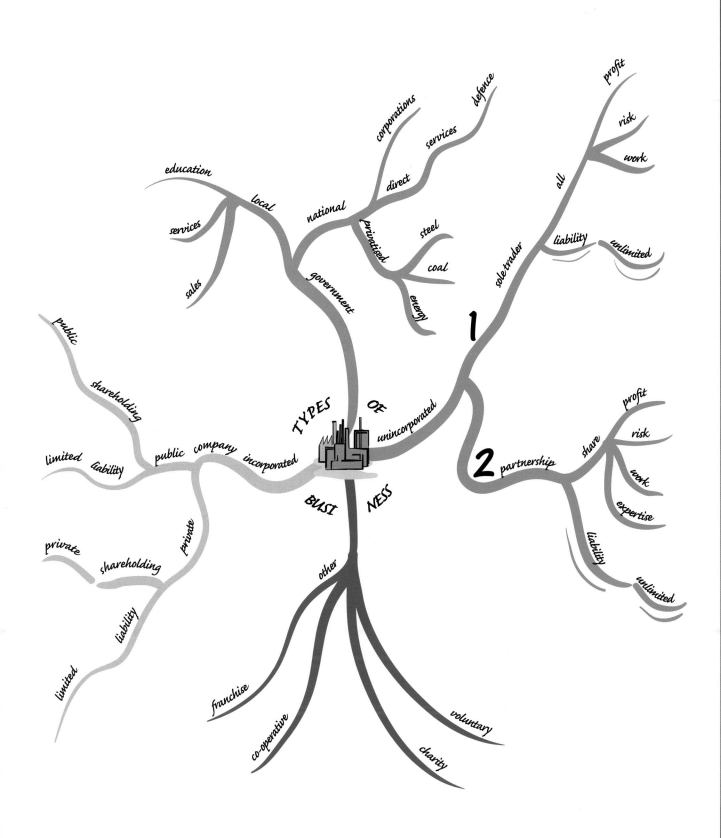

TYPES OF BUSINESS

incorporated
unincorporated

company
public
public shareholding
limited liability
private
private shareholding
limited liability

government
local
education
services
sales
national
corporations
direct
services
defence
privatised
steel
coal
energy

1 sole trader
all
profit
risk
work
liability
unlimited

2 partnership
share
profit
risk
work
expertise
liability
unlimited

other
franchise
co-operative
voluntary
charity

4 Business types

Unit 15 Sole trader

REVIEW THIS

Businesses are owned by people, and by other businesses. Some are owned by just one person, others are owned by many people. Different sorts of ownership suit different businesses due to things like the size of the

business and how much it costs to set it up. With some businesses, the owners take all the risk themselves. In return they also take all the profits. In other businesses, the owners share the risk, but will also have to share the profits.

READ THIS

Richard Branson is one of the best-known businessmen in the world. His Virgin brand is one of the best-known brands. Branson is thought to be worth around £6 billion but his first business was small. While he was still at school he decided that he could produce a better magazine for students than the ones he had seen. He set up *Student Magazine* when he was just 16 years old. This was his first business. When he set up his Virgin record business in 1970 he did not have a shop; the business sold records by mail order. Later, he opened a record shop in Oxford Street, London. This was later followed by a recording studio and the Virgin record label.

Richard Branson started *Student Magazine* on his own, as a **sole trader**, using his own money and taking the risk himself. He also had control of the business. He did not need much money to set up, so he chose the best form of business for him. The Virgin Group has now grown to around 200 companies in over 30 countries, which are owned in many different ways. The Group has expanded into music megastores, holidays and airlines, mobile phones, the internet, the drinks market and rail travel.

THE BASICS

Take a pencil or paper clip and sell it to a friend for a penny. You have just set up in business as a sole trader. That's how easy it is! You do not have to have a shop, or even a stall. You just have to sell **goods** or **services**. So all you need is something to sell, and someone to sell it to. Of course you have to get the price right: try selling the paper clip to your friend for £10 and you will see why. You also have to cover your costs. You would be daft to buy a pencil for 5p and sell it for less than that. You will want to sell it for more, to make a profit – but you may not want to make as much profit as Virgin.

You should now be able to see some of the main features of a sole trader.

- ● **It is the easiest form of business to set up.**
- ● **It is a one-person business. That person owns the business, makes all the decisions and takes all the risks.**
- ● **It may sell either goods or services.**
- ● **It is likely to be small and not cost much money to set up.**
- ● **There are many sole traders (more than any other type of business).**

So, if it is so easy, why isn't everyone a sole trader? One reason is that you have to find something that you can sell, for a profit. There may be other businesses that compete with you, so that you cannot make the sales that you need. Many sole traders will sell goods that many other shops do not sell. For instance, a corner shop may sell certain foods, or a baker may sell special bread. Many sole traders sell a service, rather than a good. Plumbers, builders and driving instructors, for instance, are often sole traders.

The other reason why some businesses choose not to be sole traders is to do with risk. If, as a sole trader, you have business debts that you cannot pay, then you can lose your personal possessions to pay the debt. This is called **unlimited liability**.

DO THIS

Think of a business that you could set up as a sole trader. What are you going to sell? Will it be a good or a service? Think about where you could run the business from. Would it be school-based, like Branson's *Student Magazine*? Will you be based at home? Do you need a shop or other buildings? What or who will be your main competition?

Draw up a spider diagram with the name of your business in the middle. Now add legs to show where your business is based, what it sells and who it is competing with.

WORD BANK

Sole trader – a business with a single owner
Goods – things you can touch (like a pencil)
Services – things you cannot touch (like banking, or driving lessons)
Unlimited liability – liability is the responsibility of the owner for the debts of the business; if it is unlimited, owners could lose their own possessions to pay debts

REMEMBER THIS

A sole trader is the easiest form of business to set up. It is owned by one person. The owner takes all the decisions and all the risk. In return the owner keeps all the profit. The biggest drawback is that if owners cannot pay the debts of the business, they could lose their own possessions.

LOOK AT THIS

Unit 16 Partnerships

REVIEW THIS

Remember that the sole trader is the easiest form of business to set up. Its biggest drawback is that if owners cannot pay the debts of the business, they could lose their own possessions. Partnerships are also very easy to set up and share the same drawback. Often a partnership is formed when a sole trader wants to expand the business and needs more help. This may be specialist help such as finance or sales skills. It may be financial help to be able to afford better stock, or premises. Partnerships are often found in specialist jobs, like lawyers or dentists, so that each can specialise and between them all areas are covered.

 READ THIS

A partnership does not have to start out as a sole trader and then expand. In many cases, the partnership will have been set up by two or more people at the very start of the business. Leeds-based law firm Watson Burton has grown from its original two partners into a large organisation in the Yorkshire region. The firm specialises in helping businesses that have fallen on hard times. It advises businesses that cannot pay their debts, and helps to make them a success again. In November 2004 the firm announced that it had taken on a new specialist lawyer who had been working at a legal practice in Hong Kong. The reason for taking on a new partner is clear. The new person can bring experience and expert advice to areas of the law that current partners do not cover. This means that the firm is made

Continued →

stronger by taking on a partner who can expand its range of services. The head of the Leeds office of the firm says, 'He is someone who truly understands ... troubled businesses and delivers real value to clients' (*Source: Yorkshire Post*, 16 November 2004)

THE BASICS

A partnership is formed when two or more people agree to own and run a business jointly. In a partnership the partners share not just the ownership of the business, but also the decision-making. Usually, they also share the work. If the business is a success, then the profits are shared between the partners. If the business falls into debt, then the responsibility for the debt is also shared. One reason why some businesses choose not to be partnerships is to do with risk. If, as a partnership, you have business debts that you cannot pay, then you can lose your personal possessions to pay the debt. This is called **unlimited liability**. It is the same as the liability for a sole trader. The only advantage of being in partnership is that you have someone who can share in the responsibility.

A partnership is about as easy to set up as a sole trader. All you have to do is to find a partner and start trading. You do not have to draw up any formal documents or agreement. But, of course, where more than one person is involved, there can be disagreements. Most partnerships draw up a formal agreement so that any problems can be settled easily. (If there is no formal agreement, the law just says that everything is split equally between the partners.)

The formal agreement is called the **Deed of Partnership**. It will cover areas such as:

- **how much money each partner will risk in the business**

- **who is responsible for each part of the business (such as sales and accounts)**

- what happens if a partner wants to leave the business

- what happens if a new partner is to be asked to join the business

- what will happen to the of the business if it is wound up.

LOOK AT THIS

James, Jez and Jill are the three members of a band. Each owns their own instrument but with money that the band has earned, they have bought other gear such as an amp, speakers and sheet music. At the moment they do not have a written Deed of Partnership.

1 If the band breaks up now, how will the assets be split?

2 If there was a Deed of Partnership, how would the assets be split?

3 Explain why it would be a good idea to draw up a Deed of Partnership.

 DO THIS

Work with other members of your class. There should be a maximum of four to a group. You are going to see how well you might succeed as a partnership. Write down all the skills and good points that you could bring to the group. Are you good with people, for instance, or good with numbers or with ICT? Make a master list of all the skills in the group. Now decide what sort of business you could run as a partnership.

You should be able to explain to the rest of your class why your business will be a success!

WORD BANK

Unlimited liability – liability is the responsibility of the owner for the debts of the business; if it is unlimited, owners could lose their own possessions to pay debts

Deed of Partnership – the formal agreement between partners

Assets – things that are owned by the business, such as stock and tools

REMEMBER THIS

Partnerships are as easy to set up as sole traders. All you have to do is to start trading as a business with someone else. You will share liability, decision-making and profits. It is better to draw up a formal agreement to prevent future problems.

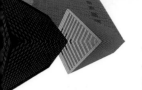

Unit 17 Limited liability companies

REVIEW THIS

Sole traders and partnerships have some really great advantages. For instance, they are really easy to set up. They also do not need much paperwork or official forms. Sole traders do not need any at all. Partnerships may choose to have a Deed of Partnership. But they both have one really big drawback. This is that the owners can lose all of their own possessions should the business not be able to pay its debts. This is called unlimited liability. There is a way in which a business can limit this liability, or responsibility for debts. This is by setting up as a **limited liability** company.

READ THIS

While setting up as a limited company has many good points, there are also drawbacks. One of the biggest of these is that, if the company is public, it can be taken over. Even if most shareholders do not want to sell, if some do, a buyer can bid for the other shares by offering to buy them. If they offer a high enough price – which will depend on how much they think the business is worth – shareholders will agree to sell. Sometimes a business will have to fight off take-over attempts.

Hit Entertainment is the company that owns the rights to children's television characters, Thomas the Tank Engine, Pingu the penguin and its

Continued →

most recent success, Bob the Builder. These characters are important assets of the company and make it attractive to buyers. If the business is doing well, then shareholders will not think of selling. If it is not doing so well, then shareholders may be keen to sell their shares. Hit Entertainment announced a 43 per cent fall in profits. Its boss then quit. Seeing this weakness, other firms at once showed an interest and Hit was forced to fight rumours of take-over bids from a Swiss firm. The people who founded Hit may really want to hang on to the business – and its children's character assets. Shareholders, on the other hand, may be less concerned with the future of Thomas, Pingu and Bob. They may be more concerned with receiving a good return on their investment!

THE BASICS

There are three parts to the name Limited liability **company**. Each is important.

- **Liability is the responsibility for the debts of the business.**

- **Limited means that this is limited to the amount of money that each shareholder has put in.**

- **Company means that the business is legally separate from its owners.**

So what does all this mean? It means that when a limited company has been set up, the owner's personal possessions are no longer at risk. It is only the assets of the company that can be taken to pay debts. The company is owned by its shareholders. All they risk is the amount of money they spend on **shares**. Shares will go up or down in value, linked to how well the business is doing. It also means that the business has its own identity in law. It is the company that owns the assets and is responsible for its actions in law. It can also be bought and sold.

Companies may be either private or public. A *private* limited company does not offer to sell shares to the public. These are often family businesses. Shares will be owned by friends and family. A *public* limited company is one whose shares have been offered for sale on the stock exchange. Both types have to go through a similar process to become a company. They must go through a set of legal formalities, including registering the company with Companies House in Cardiff. Both types also have to produce accounts that anyone can look at, so that the affairs of the business cannot be kept private.

LOOK AT THIS

Shares in Hit Entertainment

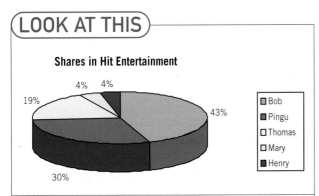

☐	Bob
▨	Pingu
☐	Thomas
☐	Mary
■	Henry

Look at the pie chart shown. Imagine that it shows how shares are owned at Hit Entertainment.

1 Who is the majority shareholder? Define what this means.

2 Explain which groups of shareholders would be able to take over the company. Explain what the shareholders need in order to be able to take over the company.

3 Swisstoys wants to take over the company. Most of the Hit shareholders do not want to sell their shares, but Pingu does. Explain the steps Swisstoys would have to go through if it still wanted to buy Hit Entertainment.

DO THIS

Draw up a table with two columns for advantages and disadvantages. At the side put 'unlimited' and 'limited' so that you can compare businesses with these types of liability. Write in as many good and bad points you can think of for each. Swap your table with a partner. See if you agree with each other, and see if you can find any more good or bad points to add.

WORD BANK

Limited liability – responsibility for the debts of the business is limited to the amount of money risked

Company – a business that is set up with a separate legal status

Shares – a share is a single part of the ownership of a company; each share has one vote when decisions are taken; each gets one share of the profits of the company

REMEMBER THIS

The most important thing gained from forming a company is to limit liability. The owners of the business can no longer lose their personal wealth to pay debts. One drawback is that it is harder to set up. Also, accounts have to be published and the business can be taken over.

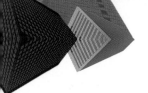

Unit 18 Franchises

REVIEW THIS

The main forms of business ownership are sole traders, partnerships, limited liability companies and the public sector (see Unit 20). Any of these forms of ownership can be used to start, run or expand a business. There are also non-profit-making organisations such as charities and voluntary groups. Remember that these are ways in which people own businesses. A franchise is *not* a different form of business ownership. Both parties to the franchise may be owned in any of the ways listed above. The business selling the franchise tends to be bigger, the one buying the franchise tends to be smaller, but there is no rule that says this must be the case!

READ THIS

Many people will recognise some major franchise businesses like McDonald's, Pizza Hut and Burger King. But franchises are not just found in fast-food businesses on the high street. They are also found in many businesses where a service is being provided. As well as offering the right to trade using a particular brand or image, franchises can also offer the right to trade in a particular geographical area.

There are franchises for some television stations. The BBC is the national broadcaster in the UK, paid for out of the television licence. Other stations are paid for by advertising or, in some cases, subscription. These are called commercial television stations. The regional stations buy a franchise to broadcast in an area for a number of years. Regional broadcasters include Yorkshire TV, HTV (Wales), Thames TV and Central.

In transport, a franchise can offer the right to run a service on particular routes. On the railways, for instance, the tracks and signals are owned by Network Rail so companies have to bid to run services and stations on them. Train operating companies include GNER, Virgin and South West Trains.

Some franchises are only for a limited period of time and can be taken away or not renewed if the terms of the franchise are not kept up. The train operator Connex, for instance, as mentioned above, had its franchise taken away because of the state of its trains and its failure to run services on time. The government took over the service.

THE BASICS

A business with a good idea, that works well, may want to expand. Of course, it can do this by opening up on new sites. It could open new branches or expand on its own site. It can also expand by selling its successful business idea to other businesses. Many people may want to start a business, but they may not have the money to risk, or the skills to run one. They may not have a good business idea.

Put the two together and you have franchising. A **franchise** is when a successful business sells the right to use its good ideas and products to other businesses. The people who buy the franchise are called the **franchisees**. They gain from using trademarks, brands and ideas that have already been tested and that work. They also gain from the support that the **franchiser** (the business selling the franchise) gives them. The franchiser gains the fee from selling the franchise and is able to expand at no cost. It also continues to gain by taking a share of the takings of the franchisee as part of the deal. This is called a **royalty**.

Continued ➔

There are drawbacks, of course. The franchisee may have to stick to certain rules and may not have much freedom to take their own decisions. The franchiser may suffer from a bad reputation if franchisees are not good enough. Connex in the south-east was so bad that it was putting people off train travel altogether. In its case, the franchiser was able to end the franchise but this is not always possible.

The franchise approach is popular because it is so successful. Over 50 per cent of other small businesses fail in their first year. With franchises, the figure is nearer 7 per cent.

REMEMBER THIS
A franchise can be owned in any of the ways in which a business can be owned. It is not a form of ownership, but a way for a business to grow. It allows a successful business to expand at low cost and a new business to start up with low risk. Franchises are also used to give a right to operate in a physical area. In such cases, they are used so that the franchiser keeps some control over quality.

WORD BANK

Franchise – buying the right to trade using the successful business ideas of another business

Franchisee – a person or business who buys a franchise

Franchiser – a person or business who sells a franchise

Royalty – a percentage share of the takings of a franchisee, paid to the franchiser as part of the deal

LOOK AT THIS

Look at the map of the UK.

1 Write down the regional transport and broadcasting franchises in, or that pass through, your area (trains, buses, TV and radio stations, for instance).

2 With a partner list all the other franchises that you know of for the other areas. (You could look in a TV guide or at travel timetables to find out.)

3 Explain why you think franchising was chosen for these businesses.

DO THIS

Design an advice leaflet for someone thinking of taking on a franchise. This should give the good and bad points of franchising. You could write the text of the leaflet using a word-processing program and then transfer it to a DTP program to make it look better.

Unit 19 Multinationals and holding companies

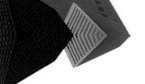

REVIEW THIS

Businesses of any type can be structured in different ways. The *structure* of a business refers to the way it is organised rather than the way it is owned. The size of the business is only one factor in deciding on how to organise it. Just because it is a big or small business does not mean it has to have a certain type of structure. The way in which a business is organised should help it to reach its aims. The main types of business in the **private sector** are sole traders, partnerships and limited liability companies. Even businesses that sound like they are not owned in any of these ways, most likely will be. So franchises (Unit 18), cooperatives (Unit 21) and other types (below) are still likely to be owned in one of these three main ways.

READ THIS

In August 2004, the Nigerian oil industry was facing big problems as workers from Shell threatened to go on strike. Royal Dutch Shell is a multinational. It is owned jointly by British and Dutch owners. It is involved in every part of oil production, from exploration through to the sale of petrol on thousands of forecourts. Shell had decided to change its structure in the country. The workers thought that this would lead to job losses, and that they would be replaced by people brought in from abroad. This would add to the losses that had already taken place due to the unrest in the oil-producing parts of the country (armed groups of rebels had threatened many Shell plants). This caused a slowdown or even stoppage of production. The government had to send in the army to put down the disorder.

Continued →

As a result of the unrest, Shell has shut down much of its production in the western area of the country. Around 2,000 barrels of oil are being lost each day due to the unrest, and about 100,000 more barrels are stolen each day from pipelines. The workers are worried that, if the situation continues, they could all lose their jobs. Shell could, if it wanted, close down all of its production and move away.

THE BASICS

Multinationals: these are businesses that produce and operate in a number of countries around the world. They gain from being able to move production and other bases to countries with lower tax rates. Often such countries also have lower rates of pay for workers. These companies tend to be **global brands**. They have outlets all over the world. Customers gain by having a product that they can buy almost anywhere in the world, but they could lose by having less choice. Countries may gain by being host to a business that provides jobs. It may also help the economy of the country. But they could lose if the business does not share skills or does not follow laws, or decides to move out.

Major multinationals include:

- **oil companies like BP and Shell**
- **fast-food companies like McDonald's and Starbucks**
- **car manufacturers like Ford and Nissan**
- **food producers like Nestlé and Kellogg's**
- **clothes manufacturers like Gap and Nike.**

Holding companies: this is a type of business that will hold all or most of the shares in other companies. All of the companies will be part of the same business group. Usually the businesses held by a holding company trade independently. They may be trading under the same name or under their own brand names. For instance, almost all businesses owned by Virgin Holdings use the Virgin name and logo. On the other hand, News Corporation Ltd (NewsCorp) uses other business names. It is the holding company for Fox News and Sky, among others. It also owns News International in the UK. This produces newspapers such as *The Times*, the *Sun* and the *News of the World*. News International is an example of another sort of company. It is a subsidiary of NewsCorp. This means that, although it runs its own day-to-day affairs, it is actually subject to the wishes of its owner – the holding company.

DO THIS

1 Richard Branson owns Virgin. Work with a partner to list as many Virgin companies as you can think of.

2 Explain why you think there are so many companies.

3 Explain the advantages to Virgin of its system of holding companies.

LOOK AT THIS

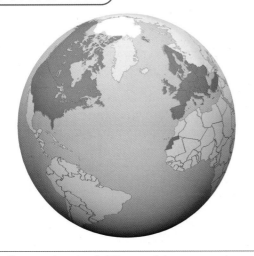

Shell operates in 145 countries around the world. Its major operations are shown above in red.

1 What advantages do you think Shell gains from operating on such a scale? What are the drawbacks? What advantages do you think the countries gain from this? What are the drawbacks?

2 Explain why the workers at Shell in Nigeria want to strike.

3 Do you think multinationals are a good or a bad thing? Explain why you think this.

WORD BANK

Private sector – businesses not owned by government, but by private owners

Multinationals – businesses that operate sales and production in many countries

Global brands – brand names and images that are recognised (and protected) all over the world

Holding companies – companies that hold shares (sometimes all of them) in other companies that are part of their business

Subsidiaries – those businesses owned by holding companies

REMEMBER THIS

Most businesses are sole traders, partnerships or limited liability companies, even businesses that may sound like they are not! Multinationals operate in many countries. They often have global brands and sales. Holding companies hold all or most of the shares in other companies. They are used as a way of keeping control of subsidiary companies.

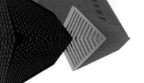

Unit 20 The public sector

REVIEW THIS

The private sector is the largest sector of the UK economy. Around 80 per cent of all jobs are in the private sector. This includes all sole traders, partnerships and limited companies. The private sector is the main employer in production and construction. It is also the provider of most service industry, such as retail sales. It includes all businesses owned by private owners. On the other hand, the public sector is the main employer in health, education and in looking after the public in general. This includes areas such as social services and the **civil service**. Most jobs are in education and the health service – around 60 per cent (according to the Office for National Statistics, 2003).

READ THIS

The office of the Mayor of London has its own transport authority called Transport for London (TFL). This has taken over some major projects that have been started by central government. Central government ministers have said that regional government, including London, should have a greater say in planning and providing rail transport. The control of the new East London Line Project was therefore handed over to the Mayor of London, Ken Livingstone, in autumn 2004. As a result of the transfer, TFL will now be in charge of a project worth over £850 million. Although this is a large project, many other public projects,

Continued →

at local, regional and national levels, involve even more money.

One of the main reasons for the public sector having to take on projects such as the East London Line is that private industry could not afford the cost. In many cases, even if it could afford it, it would not be willing to take the risk. (*Source: London Evening Standard*, 16 November 2004)

THE BASICS

Some organisations are owned and run by government. These are often businesses that are either so big or so important to a country, that private owners could not run them. Some of these are central services such as defence (the army, navy and air force) and the minting of money. Others are local services such as rubbish collection, parks and gardens, swimming pools and road mending. They are paid for out of public money. The money is collected in tax. At a local level it comes from rates and council tax. Many of these are services that no private business would try and run for a profit. How could you make a profit out of street lighting, for instance, or out of keeping footpaths clean?

In the past, many important businesses were in the public sector. These included the railways, telephone, post, gas and electricity services. Nearly all of these have now been sold into private hands. This is because the government of the day thought that private industry would run them better and save the taxpayer money. These are called **privatised industries** because they have been sold into the private sector. Each has a **watchdog** body to make sure it provides a good service and does not act against the interests of consumers.

The same has happened with certain services at local level. Where it was thought that a private company would do the job better, the service has been privatised. In most areas, for instance, rubbish collection and school meals are now in private hands. The profits from public-sector businesses go to the government or to the local authority. Many people say that this is better because everyone shares in them. Other people think that private business is better as it can be more efficient.

DO THIS

Is the meals service in your school or college run as a private or a public business? Is it owned by private owners, who keep the profits for themselves? Or is it owned by the local education authority? You are going to make a case for how *you* think it should be owned. Create a leaflet that explains all the good things about your choice of ownership.

LOOK AT THIS

Some projects that always used to be public, have been carried out by the private sector. This includes the UK's first private motorway. Draw a picture of the M6 toll road in the centre of a sheet of paper. Put all the good things about the road in one colour round your picture. Use another colour for all the bad things. Decide whether the good points outscore the bad points.

WORD BANK

Civil service – jobs in administration and in government

Privatised industry – businesses that were once in the public sector, but have been sold into private hands

Public sector – businesses owned by national, regional or local government

Watchdog – a body that watches over an industry to make sure it is being fair; they are usually called 'The Office for . . .' and this is shortened to 'Of . . .'. For instance, Ofwat is the watchdog for the water industry and Ofgas for gas.

REMEMBER THIS

The public sector is made up of those businesses and central services owned by government. They are owned on behalf of the public. Much of the public sector provides services. These include health, education and the police. In the 1970s and 1980s, much public industry was sold into private hands. Some people think private business is better. They think that if it is trying to make a profit, it will be more efficient. Other people think public business is better so that all the public can share in profits.

Unit 21 Cooperatives, charities and voluntary groups

REVIEW THIS

The aims of a business will be linked to the way it is organised. Most aim to produce a good or service to make a profit, but some have aims other than profit. In the public sector, for instance, the aim may be to provide a good service such as education, roads or health. Or they may aim to create jobs.

Cooperatives aim to bring about the most good for their members. Charities and voluntary groups aim to bring about the most good for their causes.

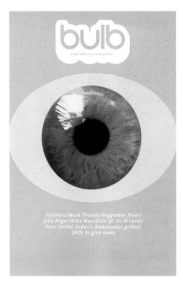

bulb

Faithless/Mark Thomas/Reggaeton fever/ John Pilger/Mike Mansfield QC on ID cards/ Fans United/Sudan's Ambassador grilled/ DVDs to give away

READ THIS

Bulb is a new magazine aimed at young people. Bulb Media cooperative is the independent, not-for-profit business that produces it. It was launched in October 2004. The people who had the idea for *Bulb* thought that teenagers might be interested in more than just gossip and pop. So Bulb Media carried out a survey to find out what were top topics for teens. Most teen magazines think that fashion, pop and gossip are the things that teenage readers are keen to read about. But *Bulb* found that 47 per cent of those who were interviewed put global issues like fair trade and justice for workers in their top three choices. *Bulb* reports on these issues, but does not ignore other issues of interest. It also has items on music, sport, fashion and gossip.

Bulb Media does not use the standard ways of getting from the press to the public. It does not use the network of newsagents. Instead there is a network of teenage sellers around the country. *Big*

Continued →

Issue is another magazine that does not use the normal channels. It is sold by street vendors. The founder of *Bulb* says '*Bulb* is about . . . working together to fight for a fairer, friendlier world. It is about ideals . . .'. The first issue looks at the decline in the numbers of voters who turn out for elections. It asks 'What's up with our democracy?'

THE BASICS

Each member of a co-op will put up equal amounts of money to start the business. Each will have an equal say in running the business and an equal share of any profits. Co-ops are a way to organise a business rather than a way to own it. Many co-ops are set up as limited companies. This protects the members.

- **Worker co-ops** produce a good or service with shared labour. This is the case with Bulb Media.

- **Producer co-ops** share in the sales of products to get a better price. They may also share costly machines. These co-ops are now common in countries growing crops such as coffee and cocoa. They help farmers in poor countries to get fair prices. Farmers markets in the UK are often co-ops.

- **Consumer co-ops** make sure members pay fair prices when buying goods and services. The first UK co-op was a consumer co-op.

- **Mutuals** provide members with financial help. Building societies were first started to help people buy houses. Insurance groups helped people to protect themselves from risk.

Co-ops are not always looking for profit. Often they just want to make sure members get a fair deal. There are other bodies that do not look for profit. Non-profit-making bodies include charities and voluntary groups.

A charity tries to make the most for the good causes it supports. As a rule, this is done by collecting money and using it to help its target group. It can also be achieved through campaigns for change. Charities must register with the Charity Commissioners. This organisation makes sure that the charity is run in a proper and fair manner. Charities also receive many tax breaks.

People work for voluntary groups for no pay. Examples include St John Ambulance and the Lions. Many voluntary groups exist at local levels.

LOOK AT THIS

People often do things for charity. They may run a race, or climb a mountain, or cycle or swim a long distance. They may also do odd things, like shave their head or dress up in costume. There are also charity auctions and events. Events range from charity film premieres to special events like the BBC 'Children in Need' night, 'Band Aid' and 'Live Aid'. Celebrities often want to be seen to be helping charities, so attend these events. They will also do things like taking part in special issues of quiz shows to raise money for charity. Why do you think so many people are keen to be involved in charity work?

 DO THIS

You are going to produce your own in-house magazine to explain the different types of business to other students.

Work in groups of three or four. Each group should produce a page that describes a type of business. Each should also give examples. The page design should be exciting and full of colour. You could look at the kind of layout used by teen magazines. Make sure that the pages are written so that your target group can understand them. When you have all finished, you should put the magazine together with a bright cover and catchy name.

WORD BANK

Worker co-ops – a group of workers join to make products

Producer co-ops – a group of producers join to achieve fair prices

Consumer co-ops – a group of consumers join to gain fair treatment

Mutuals – a group of people help each other with finance and risk

 REMEMBER THIS

Not all businesses are looking for profit. Some will have other aims. These aims may be to provide a good service. They may be to get the best deal for their members or for a target group. Co-ops try to achieve the best deal for workers, producers or consumers. Mutuals protect members from financial risk. Charities aim to raise the most money for their cause; they also campaign for change such as new laws to help people.

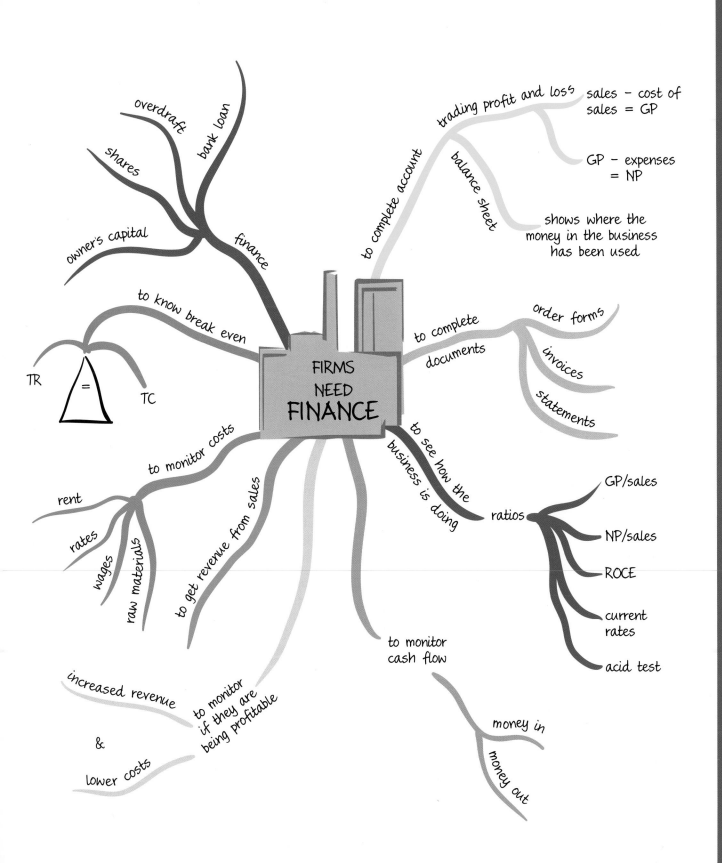

FIRMS NEED FINANCE

finance
- overdraft
- bank loan
- shares
- owner's capital

to complete account
- trading profit and loss
  - sales – cost of sales = GP
  - GP – expenses = NP
- balance sheet
  - shows where the money in the business has been used

to complete documents
- order forms
- invoices
- statements

to see how the business is doing
- ratios
  - GP/sales
  - NP/sales
  - ROCE
  - current rates
  - acid test

to know break even
- TR = TC

to monitor costs
- rent
- rates
- wages
- raw materials

to get revenue from sales

to monitor cash flow
- money in
- money out

to monitor if they are being profitable
- increased revenue & lower costs

Unit 22 The finance function

REVIEW THIS

The finance function in an organisation may be carried out by a separate department, by just one person, or by an external agency. It all depends on the size of the organisation. The largest companies have a separate department; medium-sized businesses may ask workers to combine the tasks with those from another department. In some businesses the department may be called 'accounts'. This reflects the important role of keeping records and informing the company's professional accountants of key financial figures. The name 'finance' is more often used when its roles include raising money to invest in the business.

READ THIS

In 1999 MFI, the leading furniture retailer in the UK, recognised the need to make changes to its operations if it was going to remain competitive. It started by refurbishing most of its stores, but this did not deliver the expected growth in sales. As a result, MFI had to borrow large sums of money because it suffered a large outflow of cash. This caused major problems and the company had to act quickly to change its finances. A new management team was appointed and this started to change the way the company was financed. New controls and methods were also put in place. All of this action by the finance department helped MFI to build up its cash funds, which were then available to help the company expand successfully.

THE BASICS

Whether it is called 'finance' or 'accounts', there are a number of basic functions that workers in this area will carry out. The main ones are:

- **to keep records and accounts, so that managers and owners can understand the finances of the business**
- **to give financial advice when the business is planning its various activities**
- **to pay wages and salaries correctly and on time**
- **to pay all the other bills that come into the business**
- **to make sure that the business has enough money both to meet its running costs and for any renewal or expansion**
- **to maintain accounts to meet any legal and tax requirements.**

Job roles

If you start to break down this list of functions into smaller tasks, you will begin to have an idea of the sort of job roles within the finance and accounting department. Some of the roles might be:

- **chief accountant** – this person will have overall responsibility for all of the functions listed above
- **management accountant** – this person will be specifically responsible for finding the key figures and data to help all of the main managers run the business effectively
- **credit controller** – this person will keep an eye on any money owed to the company by its debtors, and will carefully control any payments made to its own creditors
- **cost accountant** – this role is particularly important in large businesses where costs can easily spiral out of control; a major task will be trying to find ways to reduce costs wherever possible

- **chief cashier** – as the name suggests, in any business where a lot of cash (not forgetting cheques and credit card payments) is received people need to take responsibility for handling and banking money securely

- **wages clerk** – a very obvious job role, this person will be responsible for making sure that each worker receives the right pay in his/her bank account and that, of course, the right amounts of money are taken off for income tax, national insurance and pension fund contributions.

What does the finance department do?

The finance department always plays a central role in a business organisation. At the start of the business, it raises money so that trading can start. Without this money, materials cannot be bought, goods will not be produced and therefore revenue will not be earned because there is nothing to sell. As well as finding **capital**, the finance department has to produce formal accounts, including balance sheets and profit and loss accounts. These tasks are part of its function to undertake **financial accounting**.

The finance staff also have to watch over the expenditure of other areas to make sure that they do not overspend. Departments are expected to plan and keep to budgets. Watching budgets, using both cashflow forecasts and break-even analysis will form part of the finance department's other function of **management accounting**. The information the department collects will be made available to senior managers so that they can make better-informed decisions.

Most businesses appoint an outside organisation to check the accuracy of accounts. This is particularly important for the accounts that have to be produced for legal or tax reasons. The official title for someone who checks accounts is an **auditor**. The auditor checks that figures have been input

and calculated correctly. In the case of companies, the auditor has to sign the accounts to say that they are a true and fair record.

DO THIS

Either write an information leaflet aimed at young students to explain the tasks of a typical large finance department, or create a spider diagram showing the main tasks and roles of the finance department.

WORD BANK

Capital – money that is invested in a business

Financial accounting – the recording of financial information in accounts as required by the law and by the tax authorities

Management accounting – key financial information made available for management to help make decisions in running the business

Auditor – someone who carries out independent checks on the truth and accuracy of a business's financial records

REMEMBER THIS

The finance department is essential to a business, both to provide the money for other departments to operate and in controlling the financial dealings of those departments. The main functions are to obtain finance; record financial transactions; analyse costs, and prepare wages and salaries; prepare the end-of-year accounts; produce continuous financial information so that managers can run the business effectively; manage debt.

Unit 23 Raising finance

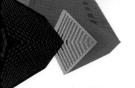

REVIEW THIS

Whether a business is being set up and then operated, or whether it is being expanded, the owners need money. They might be able to provide some of this money themselves, but most businesses need to look for additional sources of finance. Most of these sources will involve some form of borrowing. Money might be borrowed for a few days or for several years. Usually, the bigger a company is, the more sources of finance are available to it.

READ THIS

In February 2005, Nissan announced that the Cash–Ky, the replacement for the Almera, would be built at its Sunderland factory. As a result, 200 new jobs would be created and over 1,000 existing jobs safeguarded, with over £223 million being invested.

Sunderland faced competition for this model from a Nissan factory in France. The high productivity levels at the Sunderland factory helped persuade Nissan to choose it for the new model. The £5 million grant given by the UK Government towards development costs also helped to influence the choice.

THE BASICS

There are four main reasons why a business needs money to finance its activities. These are as follows.

1 **The owners of a business need money to start up their business. They need premises, equipment, stocks of materials and eventually they will need to hire workers.**

2 **They need finance to help keep the business running once it has been set up. A pool of cash will help to pay for unexpected bills. This is especially important when the flow of cash into a business slows down.**

3 **Finance is needed to renew premises and equipment after the business has been running for a while. Buildings may need to be decorated, while worn-out equipment may need to be replaced.**

4 **Finance is needed to expand the business. This might be an extension at the existing site, or the business may want to add new sites.**

How to find the money

The starting point is for new owners to look at their personal resources. They might have saved money over a few years or they might have received a lump sum if they have been made **redundant**. Family and friends might be prepared to lend money, and these days a lucky win on the National Lottery might provide suitable funds. Finding someone else to join you in the ownership of your business is another way of finding the necessary finance. A sole trader might change the business into a partnership. An existing partnership might look for additional partners or might change into a limited company. Existing companies could issue new sets of shares. Successful, profitable businesses could keep some of the profits within the business, rather than sharing them out between the owners. These **retained profits** can be used to create a cash reserve or to invest in new equipment. All of these methods will help provide **owners' funds**.

Grants are 'gifts' of money that do not have to be paid back. A wide range of grants is available to all sorts of firms. The amounts of money can vary from £50 per week for new small firms, up to many millions of pounds for large companies.

Owners' funds and grants are rarely enough to start up or expand a business. Most businesses need **borrowed funds** to top up their finances. Overdrafts are agreements with banks that allow the business to take more money out of its account than there is in it. This helps the business with cash shortages but high interest rates are charged. A 'free' form of finance is trade credit. This is when suppliers give a business up to 30 days to pay their bills.

Tool hire shop which leases equipment

Some equipment and vehicles can be leased. This means that the business does not have to put up a large sum of money at the start, but regular, smaller amounts will have to be paid out continuously. It does mean that the business can update equipment quite easily, but rent for leasing a building can be increased.

The main way to borrow money is by using loans. A lump sum is borrowed for a certain period of time and paid back with interest. These loans can last between one and twenty years. The amounts borrowed might be a few thousand pounds but, for the largest companies, might be over a hundred thousand pounds.

DO THIS

Create a four-column table. For each method of finance described above; name the method, describe it, and give the advantages and then the disadvantages.

WORD BANK

Redundant –when a worker is made unemployed because the business no longer needs that job to be done

Retained profits – part of profits that are not given to the owners, but are used as a reserve or for buying new resources for the business

Owners' funds – any money put into the business by the owners using their own resources

Grants – a 'gift' of money given by an outside body to a business, which does not have to be repaid

Borrowed funds – this involves the business going into debt and the finance has to be repaid, usually with an interest charge on top

REMEMBER THIS

Businesses need money to finance starting up the business, to help cash flow, to renew equipment and to expand. Some of the money will be provided by the owners themselves. Some money may be given as grants. The remaining money may be borrowed in some way, but has to be repaid with interest.

Unit 24 Costs and revenue

REVIEW THIS

Whether a business is making a good or providing a service, it will need lots of resources. These resources will include premises, equipment, raw materials and/or workers. The payments a firm makes for these resources are called costs of production. When the business sells its goods and services, it will earn an income. This income is usually called sales revenue. As long as revenue is greater than the costs, the business will make a profit.

READ THIS

Kent Clarke ran his own hairdressing business in Ashington, Northumberland, for over 25 years. For the first 20 years, he employed a fully trained assistant at his small salon, just down from the town's main high street. As trade slowed down, Kent was the only stylist and he hired a trainee to do the less skilled tasks. With all the competition in the town, Kent found it increasingly difficult to cover all of his **overheads** with the revenue he was earning. In 1999, after some careful research, Kent decided to close his salon. Within a month he had set up as a mobile hairdresser. His revenue fell a little as he lost some customers, but his lower running costs helped his business to become more profitable.

THE BASICS

Costs of production are the payments for buying or hiring all the resources needed to set up and run a business. For any business, the main types of resources needed will include:

- **workers**
- **land**
- **buildings**

- **power**
- **equipment**
- **communications**
- **raw materials**
- **parts and components**
- **interest on loans.**

These groups of costs hide the fact that a typical business may have over a hundred different costs. For example, hiring workers creates such costs as wages, national insurance and training, as well as all of the costs in recruiting the workers in the first place. Buildings costs might include the cost either of purchasing premises or of renting it, plus such things as insurance, repairs and business rates.

A firm planning to set up a new business often likes to identify costs under the headings of start-up costs and running costs.

- **Start-up costs** are any costs that the business has to pay out before it starts to make and sell goods or provide services. Purchasing buildings and equipment are good examples of start-up costs.

- **Running costs** are the costs a business needs to pay out for its day-to-day operations as it makes goods or provides its services. Payments for gas and electricity and wages to workers are good examples of running costs.

Of course, there are some costs that will have to be paid both to start up the business and to run it. A good example for a shop would be buying in stock before it opens for the first time. The stock would have to be replaced once customers started to buy it.

Another way to divide up costs is into those that are fixed and those that are variable.

- **Fixed costs** do not change – e.g. the rent paid for using a building or a vehicle.

- **Variable costs** do change – e.g. with the number of items you make or the number of customers served.

Sometimes a cost might be a combination of both fixed and variable costs. Heating and lighting a bread shop will be a fixed cost, but the electricity used in heating up pies will be a variable cost.

Heating up food is a variable cost

A business can calculate the **total costs** from making a good by adding up all the costs it has to pay out to make a certain quantity of **output** over a certain period of time. Quite simply it could add its fixed and variable costs together. If it then divided the total costs by the number of items it had made (its output), the business would find out how much each item cost to make on average. This is usually called **unit cost**.

Revenue is the income earned by a firm selling goods or providing services, before any costs have been taken away.

DO THIS

Think about Kent's original business set in the hairdressing salon.

1 Create a list of at least 50 costs that Kent would have had to pay, both to start up and run his business at the salon.

2 Name five of these costs that would only be start-up costs. Explain why you have chosen them.

3 Name five of the costs that would only be running costs. Explain why you have chosen them.

4 Explain why Kent might have been able to reduce his running costs greatly by changing to become a mobile hairdresser.

5 When Kent switched to mobile hairdressing, he would have had a different set of costs. Name three costs that you think would be fixed costs and three costs that you think would be variable costs. Give reasons for your selection.

REMEMBER THIS

Costs are payments by a business for the purchase or hire of resources. They may be divided up in a number of ways, fixed or variable, start-up or running. When goods and services are sold, the income earned is called revenue.

Unit 25 Break-even

REVIEW THIS

When a business first starts up or when it introduces a new product, one of its objectives is likely to be to break-even. By calculating its break-even point, the business will know the level of sales at which revenue equals costs. It will also be able to show this on a graph, so that it can predict the effects of changes in costs and changes in prices.

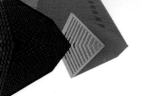

READ THIS

The new 550-seat A380 Airbus was unveiled on 18 January 2005. It is going to be the biggest passenger jetliner ever built. The likely price to buy one of these giants is £150 million. It has taken ten years and £5.7 billion to develop, with 22,000 British workers building the engines and the wings. If Airbus's figures are correct, it will need to build and sell 250 of these planes just to break even. It is only after that point that the company will start to make any profit from its investment.

THE BASICS

The **break-even point** is the level of sales where the total cost of making and selling items of output equals the total revenue from selling them. If a business sells more than this it will make a profit, but lower sales will mean that it is making a loss. This helps to show why breaking even is an important objective for most firms. Break-even can

be calculated using a formula. It can also be shown in a graph.

A break-even graph can be drawn once costs and revenue have been set out in a table. This is shown below for a national daily newspaper. The publisher of the newspaper has worked out the figures shown in the following table. Key figures are the daily fixed costs of £250,000, variable costs of 20p per newspaper and a selling price of 90p.

Number of newspapers sold (thousands)	0	100	200	300	400	500
Fixed costs (£000s)	250	250	250	250	250	250
Variable costs (£000s)	0	20	40	60	80	100
Total costs (£000s)	250	270	290	310	330	350
Total revenue (£000s)	0	90	180	270	360	450

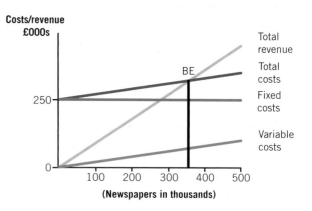

This graph shows the newspaper publisher that it needs to sell just over 357,000 newspapers each day to break even. If it sold 500,000, it would earn a profit of £100,000 each day. Selling only 200,000 a day would lead to a loss of £110,000. The graph is a good way of looking at the possible effects of changes in costs and revenue. If fixed costs or variable costs changed, the publisher could recalculate the table and then plot a new graph. It could also try out the effects on revenue of price changes.

The only problem with a graph is that it is not very accurate. To get an exact calculation of the break-even point, the **contribution** formula can be used. There are two parts to this formula.

1 **Price per unit – variable cost per unit = contribution to fixed costs**

2 $\dfrac{\text{Fixed costs}}{\text{Contribution}}$ = break even level of sales

If we use the figures for the newspaper publisher, the calculation would look like this:

1 £0.90 – £0.20 = £0.70

2 $\dfrac{£250,000}{£0.70}$ = 357,143 newspapers have to be sold each day to break even

As we have already seen, calculating the break-even point is important for all sorts of firms, not least Airbus. It gives the business a target to aim for. If the figures are accurate for the Airbus A380, any sales above 250 will start to earn the company a profit from the project. Companies can analyse their break-even graphs to see the possible effects of unexpected increases in costs. They can also plot the impact of any changes they could make to the price they charge.

REMEMBER THIS

Break-even is an important objective for many businesses but especially for new, small businesses. The break-even point will show where profits can start to be gained. It can be calculated using the contribution formula or by using a graph. Analysis of break-even can help a business to plan for possible changes and problems.

DO THIS

1 Copy out the table from the above activity and plot the break-even graph on graph paper.

2 Create a new blank table. Using the same number of sales figures, recalculate the cost and revenue figures using these values. Fixed costs fall to £240,000 per day. Variable costs rise to 25p per newspaper and the company raises the price per copy to 99p. Once you have completed your calculations, draw the new break-even graph. How does it compare to the original one?

3 Check the accuracy of the graph by using the contribution formula to calculate the exact new break-even point.

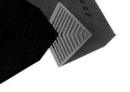

Unit 26/27 Financial documents

REVIEW THIS

Financial documents are important forms of both internal and external communication for any business. These documents help the business to keep records of its sales and its purchases. A variety of documents are used when purchasing materials, and these help monitor stock levels. Documents will also be received by the company supplying goods and services. All documents help a business to keep an accurate record of its financial situation.

 READ THIS

Kell and McGrane Ltd has been making and selling boiled sweets in the Borders area of Scotland for the past 40 years. It produces 30 different flavours of boiled sweets including pineapple chunks, raspberries and blackcurrants, and its best line rhubarb and custard. Most of its sweets are sold to wholesalers in southern Scotland. Its main purchases are sugar, flavourings and colourings bought from three main suppliers. It is vital that Kell and McGrane keeps an accurate record of its purchases and payments for these ingredients, as well as recording all its other costs and expenses. Just as importantly, it needs to keep records of all its sales. To help keep these records, Kell and McGrane uses a number of documents including purchase orders, invoices, delivery notes and goods received notes. The example of Kell and McGrane is used in this unit to explain the main financial documents.

THE BASICS

Kell and McGrane Ltd needs to buy a large amount of sugar to make its sweets. The first document it uses to buy sugar is a **purchase order**. This form requests another firm to supply Kell and McGrane Ltd with a particular number and type of good. It will be sent in the post, or perhaps by a fax machine to the supplier. Sometimes it might be a written confirmation of an order by telephone.

PURCHASE ORDER

Kell and McGrane Ltd
Borders Industrial Estate
Kelso KA4 9LT
Tel: (01234) 56789 Fax (01234) 98765

To: Canebeat Ltd
Burns Business Park
Hawick HE7 4TC

Order No: KM: 42–37
Date: 29 March 2005
Delivery: Above address

QUANTITY	REF NO	DESCRIPTION	UNIT PRICE	AMOUNT
1000 kg	–	Caster Sugar	£1.15	£1,150
			TOTAL	£1,150

Special Instructions: Please ensure delivery within 7 days of order date

Order Authorised by: J. Murray

When the sugar is sent to Kell and McGrane Ltd by the supplier, Canebeat Ltd, a **delivery note** will be sent with the sugar. This will show the exact goods being supplied by Canebeat Ltd. Most delivery notes will not include details of the price or value of the order. They will show if an item that has been ordered cannot be delivered. You will notice that signatures are required, with up to three copies of the document being produced.

DELIVERY NOTE

CANEBEAT Ltd
BURNS BUSINESS PARK
HAWICK HE7 4TC
Tel: (01456) 78910 Fax: (01456) 10798

To: Kell and McGrane Ltd
Borders Industrial Estate
Kelso KA4 9LT

Your order no: KM: 42–37
Date: 4 April 2005
Delivery no: CBD-9403

DELIVERY INSTRUCTIONS:

REF NO	DESCRIPTION	QUANTITY	NB
–	Caster Sugar	900 kg	100 kg of caster sugar to be sent within 48 hours of above date

Packed by: R Prosser   [sig]   Date: 3/4/2005
Delivered by: Fastrucks Ltd [FIRM]   Sig: P Jones   Date: 4/4/2005
Received by: P Burke   [sig]   Date: 4/4/2005

Once the delivery leaves the Canebeat warehouse, its accounts department will be asked to prepare a **sales invoice**. This is the bill for the goods that have been sent. It will include key details of the supplier – Canebeat Ltd. The exact description of the goods supplied should match the delivery note. It should also match the purchase order sent by Kell and McGrane Ltd. The invoice should clearly show the price of each item and the total value of the goods supplied. You will see on the invoice below that Canebeat Ltd expects payment within 30 days. To encourage prompt payment, it offers a small discount.

SALES INVOICE				
CANEBEAT Ltd				
Burns Business Park				
Hawick HE7 4TC				
Tel: (01456) 78910 Fax: (01456) 10789				
VAT Reg No: 987–654321				

Sold to: Kell and McGrane Ltd	Your Order No: KM: 42–37
Borders Industrial Estate	Order Date: 29/3/2005
Kelso KA4 9LT	Dispatch Date: 4/4/2005
Invoice Number: CBI–4094	Invoice Date: 5/4/2005

Ref No	Description	Quantity	Price per unit	TOTAL
–	CASTER SUGAR	1000 kg	£1.15	£1,150

Terms:	Gross Value	£1,150
Payment must be made within 30 days of invoiced date, 3% discount applies if payment received within 14 days	Less 3% discount	£34.50
	Subtotal	£1,115.50
	Plus VAT at 17.5%	–
	Invoice Total	£1,115.50

When Kell and McGrane Ltd receives the sales invoice, it will be sent to its accounts department. The department will check the invoice against the original purchase order and the delivery note. It may also check the invoice against a **goods received note**. This will be completed by the department receiving the goods. Copies will be sent both to the accounts department and the purchasing department. Once the accounts department is sure that all the details are correct it will arrange payment to be made to Canebeat Ltd.

GOODS RECEIVED NOTE			
Kell and McGrane Ltd			
GRN NO: KM/RN-4921		Supplier: Canebeat Ltd	
Date: 4/4/2005		Delivered by: Fastrucks Ltd	
Delivery Note No CBD-9403			

Order No	Quantity	Description	Ref No
KM: 42–37	900 kg	Caster Sugar	–

Received by P.Barke
Action/Comments:
Sugar deposited in main warehouse, section A.

When the accounts department at Kell and McGrane Ltd checks the sales invoice against the original purchase order and both the delivery notes and goods received notes, it will notice a problem. The invoice is for the full order for 1000 kg of caster sugar, but only 900 kg has been received. If Kell and McGrane Ltd decides to obtain the missing sugar from another supplier, the accounts department will contact Canebeat Ltd to inform it of this. To save producing a new invoice, Canebeat will issue a **credit note** to Kell and McGrane Ltd for the undelivered 100 kg. This reduces the amount of the sales invoice. The completed credit note is shown below.

CREDIT NOTE				
Canebeat Ltd				
Burns Business Park				
Hawick HE7 4TC				
Tel: (01456) 78910 Fax: (01456) 10798				
VAT Reg No: 987–654321				

To: Kell and McGrane Ltd	Date: 8/4/2005
Borders Industrial Estate	
Kelso KA4 9LT	
Credit Note No: CB/CN–421	Invoice No: CBI-4094

Ref No	Quantity	Description	UNIT PRICE	TOTAL
–	100 kg	Caster Sugar	£1.15	£115
			Gross Value	£115
			Less 3% discount	£3.45
			Subtotal	£111.55
			Plus VAT at 17.5%	–
			Invoice Total	£111.55

Once the accounts department at Kell and McGrane Ltd is happy that all the details of the transaction are correct, it will pay for the sugar. This will involve writing a **cheque** and completing a **remittance advice slip**. The cheque is a standard one issued by a bank. Large organisations have their names clearly printed on part of the cheque. The remittance advice slip matches the amount of the cheque and shows what goods are being paid for. Both the cheque and the advice slip are sent to Canebeat Ltd.

Date 10/4/2005 Canebeat Ltd	**The Eastern Bank plc**	Date 10 April 2005	55–66–77
	Pay Canebeat Ltd only		
	One thousand and three	£ 1003 - 95	
	pounds 95	B. McGrane	
		for Kell & McGrane Ltd	
£ £1003-95			
123456	123456	55–66–77	987123546

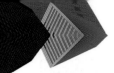
REMITTANCE ADVICE SLIP

Kell and MacGrane Ltd
Borders Industrial Estate
Kelso KA4 9LT
Tel: (01234) 56789 Fax: (01234) 98765

To: Canebeat Ltd   Our Order No: KM: 42–37
     Burns Business Park   Your Invoice No: CBI–4094
     Hawick HE7 4TC

For 900 kg Caster Sugar
Payment enclosed: £1003–95
Cheque No: 123456
Date: 10 April 2005

All queries should be addressed to the Accounts Department.

Two final documents may be created by the supplier to Kell and McGrane Ltd. Canebeat Ltd will send a **receipt** once it has received and banked the cheque from Kell and McGrane Ltd. Canebeat Ltd may also issue a **statement of account** to its regular customers like Kell and McGrane Ltd. This will show all the transactions over a period of time, perhaps a month or possibly three months. It will also act as a reminder if any bills have not been paid by Kell and McGrane Ltd. See opposite for examples.

DO THIS

Create a diagram showing the flow of documents when Kell and McGrane Ltd orders sugar from its supplier, Canebeat Ltd.

REMEMBER THIS

Purchase orders, goods received notes, remittance advice notes and cheques are produced by the purchasing firm. Delivery notes, sales invoices, credit notes, statements of account and receipts are produced by the supplier. Each document has an important part to play in making a record of transactions between firms. Accurate completion of all documents is an important requirement for all firms involved.

WORD BANK

Purchase order – used by a firm wishing to buy goods and services, and sent to a supplier with details of the goods or services required

Delivery note – used by a supplier to accompany the goods being delivered, informing the purchaser of the items being sent

Sales invoice – created by the supplier to inform the purchaser of the prices and total values of the goods being sold

Goods received note – completed by the purchasing firm to notify the ordering and accounts departments that the goods have been received in the correct amounts and in good condition

Credit note – used by a supplier when the sales invoice sent includes a value for goods that were not supplied or were not in a condition to be accepted by the purchaser

Cheques – the most common method of payment used by firms

Remittance advice slip – usually created by a purchasing firm and sent to the supplier with payment for an invoice to show exactly what is being paid

Receipt – provided by firms receiving payment for goods and services to show that a bill has been paid

Statement of account – generated by a supplier to show the value of goods being sold and the amount of money received from an individual purchasing firm over a period of time

Date _____
No _____
From _____
_____
Amount **£** _____
Cash _____
Cheque No _____
_____
Credit Card No
_____

RECEIPT

No _____   Date _____

Received from _____

Amount **£**_____

Cash _____   Credit Card No_____

Cheque Number _____

Signed _____   for Canebeat Ltd

STATEMENT OF ACCOUNT

Canebeat plc,
Burns Business Park
Hawick HE7 4TC
Tel: (01456) 78910
Fax: (01456) 10798
VAT Registration Number: 987–654321

Account name:

Account no:

Date:

INVOICE NO	DATE	DEBT

DATE	CREDIT	BALANCE

Total balance outstanding

£

TERMS
Payment must be made within 30 days of invoice date.

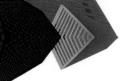

Unit 28 Cash flow forecasts and budgets

REVIEW THIS

When a business is operating, it needs to make sure that it has enough cash to pay its debts. Even though a business might be profitable, it could still go out of business if it has a cash shortage. To prevent this, a business prepares a budget. This will predict its future flows of cash, both into and out of the business. The cash flow forecast can then be compared with the actual flows of cash. As a result, the business can take action both before and when it suffers cash problems.

READ THIS

Rick Hardy has run his own building business in Northumberland for over 25 years. His main work is building extensions to people's existing houses. Rick has three full-time workers for the main building and woodwork, but subcontracts much of the specialist electrical, plastering and plumbing jobs to local firms. While his two vans are his main overheads, he has to pay for a large amount of materials, as well as wages for his workers and the fees of the subcontractors. Much of his income does not come in until a job is completed. As the average extension takes six weeks to complete, Rick has to plan his cash flow very carefully. He certainly makes use of trade credit, and has negotiated a sizeable overdraft with his bank. Where possible, he asks his customers to pay a weekly instalment towards the building costs.

THE BASICS

Cash constantly flows into and out of a business. When a business is first started, the owners are responsible for putting cash into it. They will find this from their own personal sources, but will also top it up from grants and loans. Much of this start-up capital will quickly flow out as buildings, equipment, furniture and stocks of materials are bought or leased. Once the business is running, cash will continue to flow out as workers are paid, electricity is used and more materials are bought. As soon as goods are sold or services provided, the business will start to receive cash from its customers.

The problem with the flow of cash is that the outflows and the inflows are rarely equal on any particular day, week or month. If the **cash outflow** is greater than the **cash inflow**, the business will have a **cash shortage**. This may mean that the business finds it very difficult to pay its debts. It may even find it difficult to pay its workers or to order new stocks. If the situation becomes really serious, a business might have to close down. If the flow in is greater than the flow out, the business will have a **cash surplus**. This will help to balance out cash shortages.

Successful businesses are the ones that plan for cash shortages. They produce a form of budget or cash flow forecast to predict their flows of cash. These forecasts help to show when a business might suffer from a cash shortage. This will then allow the business to take action to prevent problems.

The main items in a cash flow will look like this:

Amount in £	Month 1	Month 2	Month 3
A Bank balance brought forward	1,000	(2,000)	500
B Cash from sales	15,000	18,000	16,000
C Total cash available (A + B)	16,000	16,000	16,500
D Total cash out	18,000	15,500	17,500
E Bank balance carried forward (C − D)	(2,000)	500	(1,000)

This cash flow forecast shows that the business starts with £1,000 in the bank in month 1. Over that month, a total £15,000 of cash flows in. This means it has £16,000 available in month 1 to balance any cash flowing out. In fact, £18,000 of cash flows out, meaning that the business has become overdrawn at its bank. Its overdraft at the end of month 1 is £2,000 which is put in brackets to show it has a negative value. This also means that the business starts month 2 owing £2,000 to the bank. During that month, £18,000 of cash flows in while £15,500 flows out. As a result, at the end of month 2, the business is back in credit at the bank by £500. By the end of month 3, the business is back in the red (overdrawn) at the bank by £1,000.

The cash flow forecast above is shown as a table. The forecast can also be shown in a graph. This shows the net flow of cash by showing the bank balance at the end of each month.

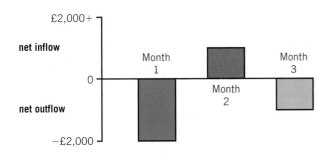

A more detailed cash flow forecast can be produced by making a list of costs. The business can then estimate figures for each of these items. As soon as the business knows the actual figures, it can update its forecast to make it more accurate.

Unit 29 Business accounts – the balance sheet

REVIEW THIS

All businesses have to produce a number of financial accounts. When a business wants to know how much it is worth, it can use its balance sheet. This account is like a snapshot, as it shows what the business is worth at a particular moment in time. The main parts of the account show what the business owns, what the business owes and the value of the money invested in the firm. The account gets its name from the rule that its figures must always balance.

READ THIS

Widegates Ltd is a private limited company operating in Morpeth, Northumberland. As an agricultural merchant, its main activity is supplying seeds, fertilisers, pesticides and hand tools to the agricultural community. It also operates a country store selling a wide range of plants, gardening equipment and general produce for those living in a rural community. It was set up by Stewart and Jane Jones as a partnership in 1985. When they decided to expand ten years later, they decided to invite a couple of friends to join them in the business. At this point they changed into a private limited company. As shareholders and managers, they all use the balance sheet, together with the other key financial accounts, as a way of analysing the progress of the company.

THE BASICS

The balance sheet is an account that gives a statement of a business's wealth on a particular date. The final version of the balance sheet is prepared at the end of a business's financial year. There are different ways to set out a balance sheet, depending on the type of business. A sole trader's balance sheet is likely to be simpler than one produced by a company. All balance sheets will have three main parts.

1 **Assets: everything that a company owns and that can be valued.**

2 **Liabilities: everything that a company owes and that can be valued.**

3 **Capital: the different forms and sources of money invested in the business.**

The layout shown in the example balance sheet below is for a private limited company. In this case it is the balance sheet for Widegates Ltd, the agricultural merchant and country store.

Extract from the balance sheet for Widegates Ltd as at 30 April 2004

	£	£	£
Fixed assets			
Land and buildings	200,000		
Equipment and vehicles	85,000		
Furniture and furnishings	15,000		
			300,000
Current assets			
Stocks	80,000		
Debtors	9,000		
Cash	1,000		
		90,000	
Current liabilities			
Creditors	11,000		
Bank overdraft	5,000		
		16,000	
Net current assets			74,000
Total assets less current liabilities			374,000
Less			
Long-term liabilities			25,000
Net assets employed			349,000
Capital and reserves			
Share capital			298,000
Reserves			10,000
Profit and loss account			41,000
			349,000

This shows that the overall value of Widegates Ltd on 30 April 2004 was £349,000. The shareholders could compare this figure to previous years to see if the company was growing in value. It might be possible to make some comparisons to similar companies, or at least to any targets that the shareholders and managers have set. Individual figures could be compared to see if there have been any important changes. In particular, the figures for current assets and current liabilities can be used to see how easily the company could meet any debts.

DO THIS

1 Copy out the Widegates Ltd balance sheet from the opposite page and use a calculator to create the balance sheet for the next financial year. Use the following figures for the year end 30 April 2005:

- the value of the land and buildings is £205,000

- the value of stock is £82,000

- debtors are £15,000; creditors are £14,000

- the profit and loss account is £51,000.

2 Compare the balance sheets for the two years and describe the changes that have taken place.

REMEMBER THIS

A balance sheet shows the value of a business at a particular point in time. It shows the value of assets owned, liabilities owed and the capital at work in the business. The balance sheet must always balance!

Unit 30 Business accounts – the profit and loss account

REVIEW THIS

When a business is set up, one of its main objectives is to make a profit. In simple terms, business profit is achieved when income is greater than expenditure. All businesses need to keep a full record of income and expenditure, and this is used to create a profit and loss account. The account looks back at business performance, usually over 12 months. It can then be compared to previous years. The accounts kept by a company are much more complicated than those kept by sole traders and partnerships.

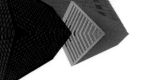

READ THIS

Lockey's Burger Bar has been open for business for over ten years. It has gradually built up business despite competition from a few national takeaway companies. At the end of each financial year, Bill Lockey prepares a profit and loss account. This shows the income he has earned from selling his burgers over the year. It also shows all of Bill's expenditure. Finally, the account shows the profit the business has made. This will be used to allow the Inland Revenue to calculate any tax that the owners have to pay on its profits. It will also help Bill and his partner to decide how much profit to pay themselves and how much to reinvest in the business. They will also be able to compare the key figures to the previous year to see if the business is improving its profitability.

THE BASICS

A profit and loss account is a record of the firm's financial record in the past. You could say it is like a historical document, but a firm can also choose to estimate its future profitability. A profit and loss account shows the main sources of income and the main items of expenditure. The figures are usually for one year. The simplest form of profit and loss account will look like the one below for Lockey's Burger Bar.

Profit and loss account for Lockey's Burger Bar for the year ending 31 July 2005.

	£
Sales revenue	550,000
Less cost of sales	220,000
Gross profit	330,000
Less expenses	270,000
Net profit	60,000

Sales revenue is the income received by Lockey's Burger Bar from selling its various burgers, chips and drinks over the 12 months ending on the 31 July 2005. The account shows that Lockey's earned £550,000, but this is not its profit because no costs have been deducted. The first set of costs that have to be deducted are **cost of sales**. These are the costs of all the ingredients and complete food and drink items that Lockey's bought in over the year. Typical items include uncooked burgers, potatoes, bread buns, sausages, cooking oil and ketchup.

The account shows that Lockey's bought in £220,000 of food and drink. When this figure is taken away from the figure for sales revenue, Lockey's will know how much **gross profit** it has made. In this case Lockey's Burger Bar has made a gross profit of £330,000. This is still not the final profit because lots of other costs, or **expenses**, have to be considered. The account shows that the business had £270,000 worth of expenses. Typical expenses are wages, rent and rates, power, insurance and equipment costs. When these are deducted from the gross profit figure, Lockey's Burger Bar makes a **net profit** of £60,000.

Many businesses will produce a more detailed profit and loss account, which shows the main expenses. A typical example is shown for Lockey's Burger Bar below.

	£	£
Sales revenue		550,000
Less cost of sales		220,000
Gross profit		330,000
Less expenses		
Wages	110,000	
Rent and rates	45,000	
Equipment	22,000	
Power	15,000	
Other	78,000	
		270,000
Net profit		60,000

So, what happens to the £60,000 of net profit? First, the Inland Revenue will collect some tax based on this profit. Second, the owners might use it to pay off loans. Third, the owners may give themselves a share of the profit. Finally, they may decide to reinvest some of the profit by buying new machinery or redecorating the premises.

Profit and loss accounts have to be published if the business is a public limited company.

REMEMBER THIS

A profit and loss account is a record of a firm's past financial performance. Sales revenue less cost of sales will show the firm's gross profit. When expenses are then taken away, the firm will show its net profit. The profit and loss account is useful to the owners, to the tax authorities and to any organisation or person thinking of investing in or lending money to the firm.

DO THIS

The following figures were taken from the profit and loss account for Lockey's Burger Bar for the year ending 31 July 2004: sales revenue – £520,000; cost of sales £190,000; wages – £115,000; rent and rates – £43,000; equipment – £18,000; power – £15,500; other expenses £77,000.

1 Use these figures to create a profit and loss account for the year ending 31 July 2004.

2 Compare the differences between the accounts for 2004 and 2005.

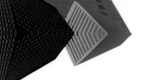

Unit 31 Understanding ratios

REVIEW THIS

When a business wants to know how well it is doing, it can look at a number of measures. One starting point is to look at individual figures from its profit and loss account and from its balance sheet. It can then look at trends in these figures and make comparisons with previous years. More usefully, a business can use figures from its accounts to calculate business ratios. Some of these ratios look at how profitable the business really is. Others look at whether a business can pay its debts.

READ THIS

Lots of different groups of people want to know how well a business is doing. Owners want to know if they are getting lots of profit for risking their money in the business. Managers want to build their reputation from running a successful company. The employees in the business will hope that their jobs are safe and that higher profits might help them get a pay rise. Any organisation that lends money will want to be sure that the business will be able to pay it back – with interest. If customers like a firm's products they will be hoping the business will continue to trade in the future. Councils and governments will want to see a business creating jobs and helping their local communities.

THE BASICS

There are lots of ways of measuring the success of a business to show how well it is doing. In this unit we will look at two ways to measure the profitability of a business, and two ways to measure the ability of a business to pay its debts.

Measuring profitability

Profitability ratios, or margins, use figures taken from the profit and loss account. The **gross profit ratio or margin** uses the gross profit and sales revenue figures. This is best shown in an example. In Unit 30 you were shown the profit and loss accounts for Lockey's Burger Bar. In the year ending 31 July 2005 its sales revenue was

£550,000, while its gross profit was £330,000. Using these figures in the gross profit ratio/margin formula:

$$\frac{\text{Gross profit}}{\text{Sales revenue}} \times 100 = \% \quad \frac{£330,000}{£550,000} \times 100 = 67\%$$

This shows that for every £100 of sales revenue, Lockey's Burger Bar was earning £67 gross profit.

The same process can be used to calculate the **net profit ratio or margin**. In 2005 Lockey's earned £60,000 from its sales revenue of £550,000. Using a similar formula:

$$\frac{\text{Net profit}}{\text{Sales revenue}} \times 100 = \% \quad \frac{£60,000}{£550,000} \times 100 = 10.9\%$$

This shows that for every £100 of sales revenue, Lockey's Burger Bar made a net profit of £10.90.

Measuring ability to pay debts

Being profitable is a very important measure of success, but if a business cannot pay its debts, it will fail. One way of measuring a firm's ability to pay its debts is by calculating its **current ratio**. This takes figures from the balance sheet. For example, in Unit 29 you were shown the balance sheet of Widegates Ltd. Two important parts were the current assets and the current liabilities. In that balance sheet, ending 30 April 2004, Widegates Ltd had current assets worth £90,000 and current liabilities worth £16,000. Using these figures, the current ratio for Widegates Ltd would be:

$$\frac{\text{Current assets}}{\text{Current liabilities}} : 1 \quad \frac{£90,000}{£16,000} : 1 = £5.63 : 1$$

This shows that Widegates could pay its current liabilities or short-term debts more than five times over using its current assets. This suggests that Widegates is in a very strong position.

The only problem is that a large part of its current assets are stocks. While some of these stocks could easily be sold for cash to pay debts, Widegates might not be able to sell enough if debts are really large. This is why some businesses use the **acid test ratio** to measure the ability to pay debts. Using the figures for Widegates Ltd, we see that £80,000 of the current assets were its stocks. Putting this into the acid test ratio we see:

$$\frac{\text{Current assets} - \text{stock}}{\text{Current liabilities}} : 1 \quad \frac{£90,000 - £80,000}{£16,000} : 1 = £0.63 : 1$$

This shows that Widegates is in a weaker position. It has only 63p to meet its short-term debts if it is unable to sell any stock. Of course, Widegates is likely to be able to sell some stock to find cash to pay for debts.

As a general rule, healthy current ratios are between 1.5:1 and 3:1. Healthy acid test ratios are supposed to be between 0.5:1 and 1:1. If we apply these to Widegates Ltd, its acid test ratio is sound, but its current ratio suggests it has too much money tied up in stock.

Unit 32 Improving profitability

REVIEW THIS

When a business has reviewed its profitability, it might decide to improve its performance. There are lots of ways for a business to improve profits. Reducing costs obviously helps to push up profits. The business might also look at methods to raise revenue such as changing prices and using different forms of promotion. Introducing new goods and services might help profits, as might an expansion of the business. Most businesses use a mix of methods to improve profits, but they would be wise to think through the possible effects of each method.

READ THIS

In the last five years, there has been a revolution in the coffee shop market. Costa, Coffee Republic, Starbucks and Caffè Nero have all led the way by opening new shops and offering speciality mugs of coffee. Alongside this, their use of comfy seating, outside tables and new ideas in snacks have been geared towards attracting and keeping custom. So why are these coffee chains having so many problems in making reasonable profits? Are their costs too high? Are their prices too low? Is there not enough custom or are customers happy to go anywhere as long as there is an empty seat? What can these coffee shops do to improve profitability?

THE BASICS

Any action that a business takes to improve profitability will have possible advantages and disadvantages. Before deciding what action to take, therefore, a business has to weigh up the benefits against the costs. The actions themselves can be grouped into four types.

Reduce costs

Most businesses should be able to improve profitability if they reduce costs. This is often the first option since it carries the least risk. It is particularly important when a business is facing a lot of competition. Some businesses have more chance of cutting costs than others. This will depend on the size of the business, whether it is a manufacturer or a service provider, whether it has a lot of costs tied up in building and equipment, or whether it has a large workforce. The overall aim is to reduce the unit cost of producing each good or service. There are several groups of costs that a business could target, including:

- rent and rates on property and land
- wages, salaries, bonuses and training costs of the workforce
- the cost of utilities such as power and water
- repair, maintenance and replacement of equipment
- repair, insurance, fuel and maintenance on transport
- all forms of promotion, including advertising
- administrative costs such as phone calls and postage
- the interest costs of its finance
- the costs of buying and storing stocks
- other overheads such as insurance.

Increase revenue

Once costs are at a minimum, a business will need to consider how to raise profits by increasing revenue. Changing the price at which each good or service is sold is one possible action. A higher price for an item will mean that each one sold earns more revenue. But will the business sell as many? A lower price will probably attract more custom but each one will earn less profit. Before changing price in either direction, the business will need some information about its customers. Are they attracted by bargains or are they prepared to pay a little more to get their preferred brand? One other thing to consider is how competitors will react. Few businesses want to get into a price war where each tries to undercut the other.

Increase sales

Finding ways to increase sales is therefore a more attractive option than changing price. This is where the business needs to use advertising and other promotional tactics. Packaging, gifts, money-off coupons and free samples are examples of promotional tricks used by business. The problem with advertising and promotion for a business is that both will cost money. So before they are used, the business will have to be sure that the extra revenue gained will at least cover any extra costs.

New products

Another marketing tactic used is to introduce new products. Sometimes the 'new' products might just be a repackaged version of the old one. Films on DVD and books sometimes have a new cover that can fool customers into thinking that they have not bought the item in the past. Some products are improved versions, such as cars with extra features or soap powder with a special ingredient. These tactics try to extend the life of such products. In the end, though, the producer has to bring out a new product. A good example of this is the car industry when a manufacturer brings out a completely new model; for example, Citroën replaced its old small car, the Saxo, with a completely new model named the C2, below.

Sometimes, a business may have to move into completely new and different markets if it wants to improve profitability. This is often called **product diversification**. The business might find that the market for its original product is beginning to contract. For example, some of the leading tobacco companies found this in the 1970s as people became more aware of the health risks of smoking. As a result, the tobacco companies merged with or took over companies with no links whatsoever to its **core product** – tobacco.

 DO THIS

Your local burger bar or fast-food outlet is suffering from falling profits. Think of six actions it could take to improve profitability. Write down the possible costs and benefits of each action. Decide which action or actions you think would be best for that business.

WORD BANK

Product diversification – moving resources into products and markets that the business has not been involved with before

Core product – the original and/or main product of a business

REMEMBER THIS

Profits may be improved by reducing costs, by increasing revenue, by introducing new products or services, or by a general expansion of the business. Each method of improving profits is likely to have both costs and benefits to the business. Before deciding which action to take, a business needs to weigh up the likely costs and benefits of each.

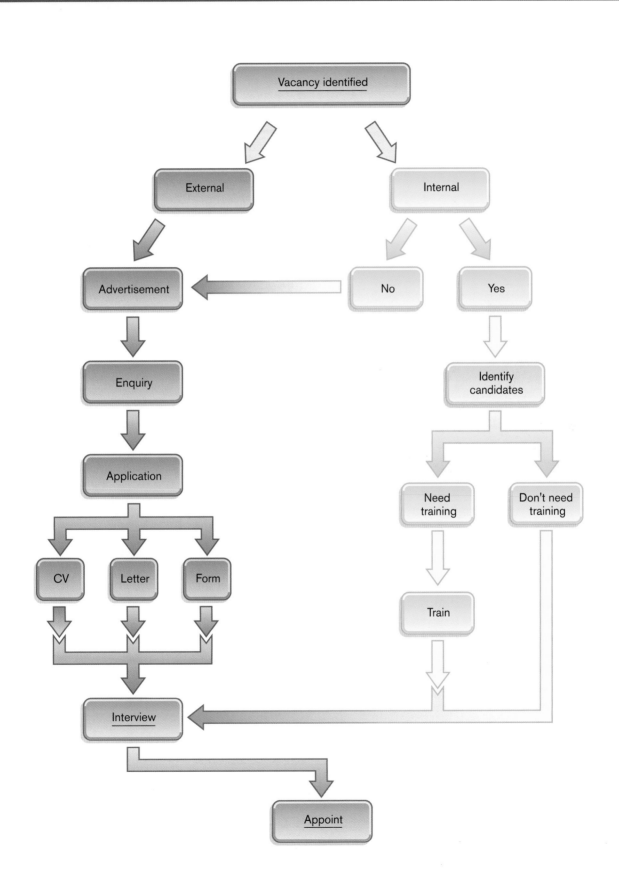

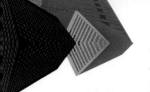

Unit 33 Human resources function

REVIEW THIS

Businesses need many types of resource in order to succeed. They may need raw materials, tools and machines. They need a place to operate from. They need money to buy the resources. One of the most important things that all businesses need is good people. The human resources function is that part of a business that deals with people. It hires the workers that are needed and has the job of getting rid of workers if they are no longer needed. But it doesn't deal only with hiring and firing; it deals with all the aspects of a worker's relationship with a business.

READ THIS

In October 2004, the human resources area at HSBC bank moved 4,000 jobs out of the UK and into India. This is not as easy as it sounds. It means making redundant all the workers no longer needed in the UK. It also means having to recruit and train 4,000 workers in India. One research body (Deloitte Research, 2004) thinks that this is just the start of a trend, and that over two million jobs from around the world will end up in India in the next few years.

The jobs that are being created in India are in call centres. So why should a business go to so much trouble just to move a call centre halfway around the world? Of course, it does not matter where a call centre is actually based, as long as

Continued →

the call charges are lower. Using places such as India would never have been possible without the huge fall in call charges from such countries. With changes in technology, call charges are no longer an important factor. Phone charges from India have fallen from 60 rupees a minute in December 2000 to under 10 rupees a minute in December 2004 (this is about 11p in UK terms). Wages, however, are also a factor. They are much lower than in the UK. A call centre worker in the UK could expect to be paid around £18,500 per year. In India, the rate is just £2,500 a year. But the workers in India are not being badly paid. In their country, this is a really good wage to be earning. It is four times the wage that the average teacher earns. (*Source: the Guardian*, 17 November 2004)

THE BASICS

The **human resources function** is in charge of everything to do with the people that are employed in a business. The areas it deals with include pay, pensions, holidays, disputes, discipline and training. In a large business, there could be separate departments for each of these. In a small business, they may all be carried out by just one person. In a sole trader business for instance, it is the owner who will be in charge of all these aspects of both his/her own 'employment', and that of any staff.

Human resources will need to find out about the work that needs to be done. It can then make sure that it recruits the staff who can do the job. This means hiring the right number of staff, with the right skills, experience and qualifications. If it appoints the right staff, and keeps them happy, then it should not have to recruit too often. **Labour turnover** measures the rate at which staff leave and new staff have to be recruited. If this is high, then it shows that the business is not treating staff as well as other businesses. Perhaps it is working them for longer hours? Or not paying as well?

Human resources is in charge of workers while they are employed. It makes sure that they get the right holidays. It makes sure they get their rights, such as **sick pay**, **maternity leave**, and **paternity leave**. It deals with any arguments or disputes.

If workers leave, human resources has to send on their employment records. If they retire, it looks after their pension. It also deals with workers who are fired or made **redundant**.

LOOK AT THIS

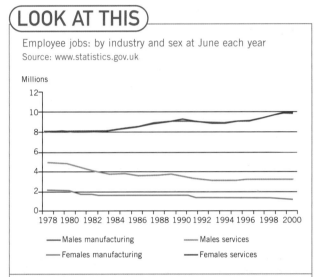

Employee jobs: by industry and sex at June each year
Source: www.statistics.gov.uk

Millions

— Males manufacturing   — Males services
— Females manufacturing   — Females services

The graph shows the changes in job patterns for the last few years.

1 Describe the general trend for each group shown.

2 Explain why you think the trend is in this direction.

3 What do you think could happen in the future if the trend for service jobs to go abroad continues? Explain your answer.

 ## DO THIS

Work in a small group of three or four people. Imagine that you are the human resources area of a major bank. You have decided to move your call centre abroad. You are going to make 5,000 people redundant in the UK. You are going to employ 5,000 new people in India.

1 Write an advertisement to recruit workers in India.

2 Write a letter to all of the people you are making redundant, explaining why you have to let them go. Suggest ways in which you could help them to get other jobs.

3 Write a training programme for your new employees.

 ## WORD BANK

Human resources function – the part of a business that deals with the workers in the business

Labour turnover – measures the rate at which workers leave a business

Sick pay – the pay you are allowed when you are ill

Maternity leave – the paid leave allowed for mothers who have just had babies

Paternity leave – the paid leave allowed for men who have just become fathers

Redundant – when a worker or their job is no longer needed

 ## REMEMBER THIS

The human resources function is just one area of a business. It has to link with all the other functional areas to be efficient. It is the area that looks after all the needs of the business as far as its workers are concerned. It also looks after all the needs and problems of the workers.

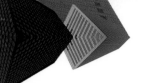

Unit 34 Pay and benefits

REVIEW THIS

The human resources function is responsible for all the areas vital to workers. It recruits them. It looks after them while they are employed. It makes sure they are treated fairly when they leave. Of all the jobs of human resources, the most important one is probably making sure that people are paid. The central concern for most workers is that of pay.

Contract caterer

Workers need to know that they will definitely be paid. They need to be paid on time, at the correct rate. That rate needs to be fair. If any of these fails, workers will look for jobs elsewhere.

READ THIS

The National Health Service is set to bring in sweeping changes to levels of pay. It is hoping to reward people more fairly for their skills. This new deal is called 'Agenda for Change'. The new deal will also give people better pay if they are willing to try more **flexible working**. The deal could produce pay rises of between 15 and 17 per cent for the lowest-paid workers. Under the deal, the health service minimum wage would rise from £4.85 an hour to £5.88 an hour.

But the deal has come with a problem. The wage rises apply only to those staff that are directly employed by the health service. A number of people working in the health service now work for private firms. These firms have bid for contracts to carry out many hospital services. These include many cleaning, catering and laundry services. These firms say that they will not be able to afford to pay the increased wages. This means that there will be two different rates

Continued →

of pay in the health service: a higher rate for direct employees and a lower rate for employees working for firms with contracts. So people could be doing the same job but being paid differently. The workers do not think that this is fair and have asked their union, Unison, to try to solve the problem for them. The **CBI** (Confederation of British Industry) is the body that represents employers. It says that the new wage rates are also a problem for its members. It would like the government to fund increases in pay for all the workers. (*Source: Financial Times,* 29 November 2004)

THE BASICS

One of the most important things to workers is how they are paid. The human resources function will decide this. General rates of pay for a job may be decided by the number of people who are willing and able to do the job. So if the job does not need many qualifications or much experience, rates of pay are likely to be low. If it is a hard job, or one that involves danger, then fewer people will be willing to do it and rates of pay will rise. Rates of pay will also be higher if people have to train for a long time, or pass exams. There are also different types of pay. The main difference is between **wages** and **salaries**.

- **A wage is paid at so much per time period (an hour, a week) or per piece of work finished (piece work). Workers who are paid a wage can normally earn overtime, at a higher rate, for extra work.**

- **A salary is paid at so much per year. This is usually paid in 12 monthly payments. Workers who earn salaries are usually expected to 'do the job' however long it takes, and do not get paid overtime.**

Different jobs also carry different benefits. These include:

- **financial benefits such as staff discounts at**

shops, free transport, canteens, a company car, annual bonus and  profit sharing schemes

- ○ job-related benefits such as training, protective clothing, and pension and health care schemes
- ○ status benefits such as a car parking space, a big office or first-class travel.

LOOK AT THIS

Look at the people in the picture.

1 Describe the job that each person carries out. Which job do you think is the most important?

2 Estimate what each person earns. List the sort of extra benefits that you think each person receives.

3 Do you think that the pay that each person receives is fair? Give reasons for your answer.

 DO THIS

Draw up a five-column table with the headings 'job', 'has to ...', 'pay', 'should be paid' and 'reason'. List at least ten different jobs. (You could use the ones in the picture as a starting point.) Under column 1 give the job name. Under column 2, describe what the person has to do in the job. Under column 3 put what you think the person earns. If you are not sure, you can use the internet to find out. In the other two columns write in what you think they should be paid, and why. Compare your table with a partner's. Do you agree?

 REMEMBER THIS

The human resources function looks after all the needs of the workers in a business. The most important thing to many workers is their pay. Human resources has to make sure that it provides the correct pay and benefits.

Unit 35 Recruitment, training and retention

Vodafone office in Newbury, Berkshire

REVIEW THIS

Workers work for businesses. Businesses need to employ workers. Human resources looks after both. It looks after the workers' needs in relation to the business. It also looks after the needs of the business in relation to workers. So good recruitment and selection is vital. This makes sure of two things. It ensures that the business employs the workers that are right for it. It also ensures that the workers are happy with the business. Good human resources is not only about taking on top staff. It will also be involved in making sure staff are kept happy, so that they stay with the business.

READ THIS

Businesses that are very good at what they do can win awards. Vodafone won an award in 2004 for being the best able to 'attract and keep top talent'. The award was made by the magazine *Management Today*. The judges were impressed by how well Vodafone looked after its staff. People from many backgrounds are employed by Vodafone, with varying levels of skills and learning. The business has set up academies so that all staff members can become as technically good as each other. The academies also help develop managers of the future, spotting the best staff so they can be quickly promoted.

Continued →

Vodafone believes in providing the best for its workers, both in the workplace and outside. For instance, there is its new office building in Newbury, Berkshire. The building is state of the art. It will house 3,000 workers. As well as being a light and airy workspace in a modern setting, it has coffee bars, a restaurant and even a gym. On the social side, all workers are invited each year to a ball, with live music from top stars. In the past Robbie Williams, Sheryl Crow and Sir Elton John have performed. (*Source: Management Today*, December 2004)

THE BASICS

Recruitment is the process by which a business finds new staff. There are a number of reasons why it might need new staff. The business could be getting bigger. Staff could have left. The business may need new skills. In such cases it has to decide whether to recruit or to train its own staff.

The next stage is to advertise **vacancies**. It is important that this is done in the right place. People who apply for a job are called **applicants**. Applicants will say why they should have the job. They can do this in a letter or by providing a CV that shows they can do the job. For some jobs, a phone call may be enough.

Human resources then goes through the **selection process**. It chooses the applicants it thinks are most likely to be good at the job. It invites them to interview. Interviews could be one to one, or in front of a panel. People coming to an interview are called **candidates**. The interview might even involve relevant tests to show that the candidate can really do the job. At the interview, or usually sometime afterwards, the best candidate is offered the job. If the candidate accepts, s/he is then appointed.

Recruiting is expensive. If a business can cut down on the number of people it recruits, this keeps costs down. This is called **retention**. It can do this by offering pay and working conditions that make staff want to stay. It can also provide good training. Training to show a new person what to do is called **induction training**. Other training may help workers to be promoted.

LOOK AT THIS

Look at 'Read This' and the picture of the Vodafone building. Think of a job that you would like to do. On a large sheet of paper, design the 'perfect' workspace for this job. Think about the sort of facilities that workers would need and about the sort of things they might want. For instance, they might need fast internet access, or a mobile phone, or a training room. They might want a gym, or a social area, or coffee bars.

DO THIS

Induction training is used to introduce new workers to a business. It introduces them to their new workmates. It tells them what they need to know about basic things, like breaks and lunch. It shows them what they are expected to do in the job. It may include training on machines; for instance, an office worker may be shown how to log on or how to operate a photocopier.

Choose a job that you would like to do. Write up a one-day induction training programme for the job. To do this properly, you will have to find out details of the organisation of the business, and how it operates. Share your programme with a partner. Do you think they have left anything out? Do they think you have?

WORD BANK

Recruitment – the process by which a business finds new staff

Vacancies – when a job is available, it is called a vacancy

Applicants – the people who apply for the job

Selection process – choosing a person from those who apply; first, choosing who to interview, then choosing who is best at the interview

Candidates – the people chosen to be interviewed

Retention – when a business keeps the good staff that it already has

Induction training – training to introduce new staff to the business

REMEMBER THIS

Businesses need new staff as they grow, or as old staff leave. Once they have identified what is needed, they advertise. People then apply. A selection process is used to find the best person for the job. This often involves a letter or CV, and then an interview. Businesses may also need new skills. In this case they must decide whether to train staff or appoint new people. By having good training and good conditions, businesses can retain staff and therefore keep recruitment costs down.

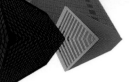

Unit 36 Applying for a job

REVIEW THIS

The process of advertising a job and appointing someone is what a business does to fill a vacancy. To mirror this, there is a process that the person who wants the job has to go through. This is the process of applying for a job. What would you do? First you would have to find a job that you could do. Then you would follow the instructions to apply. Perhaps you would need to write a letter. You would almost certainly need a CV – this stands for 'curriculum vitae', which literally means 'the story of your life'. Below is Will Smith's story. Could you make a CV from this?

READ THIS

Will Smith is a well-known singer and actor. He was born on 25 September 1968 and is one of four children. He graduated from West Overbrook High School in 1984. He later won a scholarship to M.I.T. (a top US college) but turned it down in favour of a singing career. At school, he got the nickname 'Prince' due to the way he could charm his way out of trouble.

He met his rap partner Jeff Townes at a party. They formed the duo DJ Jazzy Jeff and the Fresh Prince. In 1989 they received the first ever Grammy award for Best Rap for the song 'Parents Just Don't Understand'. (The Grammy awards are the 'Oscars' of the music business.) In 1989, he met a television producer who had an idea for a sitcom based on his own life. This led to the show *The Fresh Prince of Bel-Air*. This was first aired in 1990 and ran for six years. In 1991 he won a second Grammy, for the song 'Summertime'.

Smith is also a film actor. His first hit role was in *Six Degrees of Separation* in 1993. Also in 1993,

Continued →

he was invited to host a gala for the incoming US President, Bill Clinton. His first big movie hit was *Independence Day* in 1996. Perhaps his most famous films are the *Men in Black* movies, for which he also wrote some of the music. In March 2002, he became the first rap singer to be nominated for an Oscar. This was for his role in the film *Ali*. His latest film is *I, Robot* (2004).

In 2003 he was dropped by his record company. At 34, he was thought to be 'too old' for the young music scene. Smith enjoys playing chess and speaks fluent Spanish.

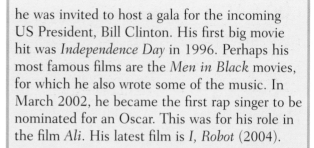

THE BASICS

What are you able to do? What are you best at? What do you enjoy doing? These are all questions you will need to ask when you are looking for a job. To apply for a job, you first need to find a vacancy. You could look in the job pages of the paper or at a JobCentre. Some vacancies are advertised on websites or noticeboards outside businesses.

Once you have found a vacancy, you then have to follow the steps that the business wants. You may have to phone for details. You may be asked to write a **letter of application**. You may be sent an **application form** to fill in. You are very likely to be asked for a CV. A **curriculum vitae** tells the story of your life. It states when you were born and how old you are. It lists the qualifications that you have, or are hoping to get. It lists the things you are good at. It may also include hobbies or other skills you have if these show your good points.

A good CV could help you to an interview. A business cannot interview all the people who apply, so it picks only the ones with the best letters and CVs. This is called a **short-list**. Those on the short-list are then interviewed.

Look at the picture. What do you suggest that the person above should wear for a job interview?

1 Describe how he should look.

2 Make a list of the sort of clothes you think that he should not wear. Describe what else he should not do at an interview.

3 Explain why interviewers want people to dress in certain ways.

 DO THIS

1 Create an application form for a chosen job. You could use word processing or DTP. The form should ask for all the personal details the business would need to know. It should have space for qualifications and experience.

2 Get a friend to test the form so that you can see if you have included all that is needed. A partner should now use the form to apply for the job. You should apply for the job your partner has chosen.

3 Write a comment on how you would improve either form.

 WORD BANK

Letter of application – a formal letter setting out why you would be the best person for the job

Application form – a form provided by the business to make sure that it collects the information it needs; it also makes applications easier to handle

Curriculum vitae – the 'story of your life', which shows that you have the qualifications, skills and qualities that an employer wants

Short-list – the applicants the business decides to invite for interview

 REMEMBER THIS

You can only apply for a job when you find a vacancy. You will need to look in the right place for this. You then need to find out what skills and qualifications are needed and make sure that you have them. To apply, you should follow the steps the business lays down. This usually means a letter and CV, or a form to fill in. You will then need to dress properly for the interview. If you are confident, know your stuff and interview well, you have a good chance of being offered the job.

Unit 37   Rights and responsibilities at work

REVIEW THIS

A business will do its best to recruit good staff. It goes through a thorough process to make sure that it has the best. When staff first arrive, they are introduced to the business. This is often part of induction training. This training will also tell staff what is expected of them. Workers have certain rights. They also have certain responsibilities.

READ THIS

One of your rights at work is to be treated equally with other people. You should be treated the same whatever your race or religion, whether you are married or not, or whether you are male or female (your gender). There are now laws to make sure that this happens.

This was not always the case. When Stephanie Shirley was trying to set up her own business in the 1960s, she found that she was being ignored. She sent letters out to people who might invest in her software company, but could not attract any interest. Stephanie wondered why this was, and decided that it was because she was a woman. At that time, women were very much expected to be housewives. Running a business was thought to be a job for a man. So Stephanie started to sign her letters as 'Steve' and did not let the people that she was writing to know that she was a woman. Straight away, she started to

Continued →

receive positive replies and her business took off. Her company is called Xansa. It is now one of the most successful software companies in the country. It is worth over £300 million. Steve, as she still calls herself, only employed female directors when she set up the business. She does now appoint men, but there are still female directors on the board. (*Source: Independent*, 8 September 2004)

THE BASICS

Both **employers** and **employees** have rights and responsibilities. Many of these are laid down in law. Most laws relate either to the health and safety of workers, or to fair and equal treatment. Businesses have to make sure that workers are not put at risk. This means providing safety signs and gear. Working areas must also be kept safe. In return, workers should not put themselves at risk by acting in an unsafe way. Safety in the workplace is covered by the law called the **Health & Safety at Work Act**.

There are laws to make sure that workers are treated fairly. These are for the good of both the workers and the employers. Workers owe a duty to their employers. They should be on time, do the job correctly, be honest and do nothing to harm the business. In return, employers should pay them the correct rate for the job. They should treat workers fairly and with respect.

A **contract of employment** is issued to make sure that both sides know what is expected of them. This includes all the details of the job. It will also include details of what action can be taken by either side if the contract is broken. The employer may be able to use a **disciplinary procedure** if the worker is at fault. The worker may be able to use the law if the employer is at fault.

The main laws say that employers are being unfair if they treat any person differently due to their:

- gender
- race or religion
- disability.

This is called **discrimination**.

LOOK AT THIS

Ben and Tim are having fun throwing the wet sponges at each other, and are caught by a foreman. Work with three other people. Two of you should be 'Ben and Tim', one should be the foreman, one should be the boss.

1 Role-play what happens when the foreman takes the boys to the boss.

2 Explain what you think should happen to Ben and Tim.

DO THIS

Steve had to pretend to be a man to receive support in starting her business. This was because women were discriminated against. Draw a spider chart or mind map with the word 'discrimination' in the middle. Add examples of the types of discrimination. Add the names of the laws that protect people from discrimination. Find an example of each type of discrimination. This might be in a textbook. It might mean looking in the library, or looking at websites. Add a slogan or catchphrase that could be used to reduce discrimination.

WORD BANK

- **Employers** – people who employ workers, often called bosses
- **Employees** – people who are employed, often called workers
- **Health & Safety at Work Act** – also called HASAW; the law that makes sure that places of work are kept safe and workers protected
- **Contract of employment** – tells workers their pay and the conditions under which they will work; it must be given to workers within 13 weeks of them starting the job
- **Disciplinary procedure** – action the boss can take if workers are at fault or break their contract
- **Discrimination** – treating someone in an unfair way due to something that has nothing to do with the job; for instance, gender, race or disability

REMEMBER THIS

Workers owe a duty to bosses to do the job correctly and behave in a proper way. Bosses have to keep workers and workplaces safe. The contract of employment is used to show what each side has agreed to. Bosses also have to be fair to workers. There are laws in place to make sure that workplaces are healthy and safe. There are also laws in place to make sure that workers are not treated unfairly.

Unit 38 Industrial relations

REVIEW THIS

Employers and employees have to work with each other. They must be fair to each other. There are laws to protect both sides if it looks like someone is not being fair. Sometimes disputes arise that cannot be solved as the

Digital print machine

two sides do not agree on the solution. In this case there are bodies that act for workers and employers. These bodies, which act for a group, have more power than just one person. Such disputes can also damage the economy. This is why the government also provides ways of settling them.

READ THIS

Kodak has seen sales of photo prints fall very quickly since digital cameras became more popular. With an ordinary camera, you have to send your film away to be printed. You have to wait quite a while for it to be developed. You also run the risk of photos being spoilt or lost in the post. With a digital camera, many people do not bother to print photos at all. They just save them to CD or to a hard drive. You can print photos at self-service booths in shops, so that you do not have to wait for the photos. It also means that, with photos not having to be sent away, there is no risk of them being lost in the post.

As a result of this, Kodak plans to close six UK photo printing labs and a call centre in 2005. It has already said that it is axing 600 jobs and closing a plant in Nottingham with a further 350 job losses. Trades unions representing the workers will work to make sure that their members who are made **redundant** receive a fair deal, the best deal possible from the company. They will try to make sure that **redundancy benefits** are paid and that workers receive help to find new jobs. (*Source: Yorkshire Post*, 18 November 2004)

THE BASICS

Sometimes, even though there are contracts of employment, there can be disputes between employers and employees. When these disputes are about work, they are called **industrial disputes**. **Industrial relations** is the term used for the dealings between worker groups and employer groups. **Trades unions** are the bodies that act for groups of workers. They were first set up to make sure that workers had decent pay and working conditions. They still fight to improve these. For instance, trades unions supported the introduction of the minimum wage. They are also working to persuade employers to give workers more of a say in business decision-making. Employer associations act on behalf of employers. The body that acts for many employers is called the **CBI**. This stands for Confederation of British Industry.

Most disputes are solved inside the business, by following the steps laid down in contracts. They may also be solved by **collective bargaining**. If a dispute is not solved in this way, workers may take action to try to force the employer to give way. This action might mean:

- refusing to work overtime
- working slowly (a 'go-slow')
- following all the rules in a detailed way so that work is slowed down (working to rule).

The very last resort is for the union to tell its workers to stop working. This is called **strike action**. Most disputes do not reach this point. The two sides can agree that an outside body decides the issue. The main outside body is **ACAS**, which offers advice to both sides. It also says whether workers who think they have been unfairly treated can appeal to an employment tribunal.

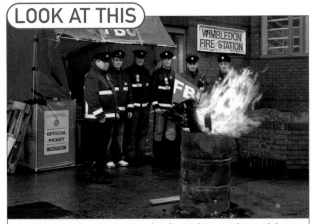

A dispute is really bad when it reaches this stage. It means that employers and employees have failed to agree on how to solve a problem. It is now rare to see disputes get as far as strike action.

1 What sort of a dispute do you think is taking place? What could be the main cause?

2 Outline the steps that could be taken if such a dispute happens.

3 Explain why the dispute might have reached this serious stage.

 DO THIS

Imagine that you are one of the workers that Kodak is making redundant. You have worked for Kodak for ten years.

1 Find out what rights you have. For instance, how much notice should you be given? How much pay should you receive?

2 Describe which of these rights you have by law. Describe how trades unions helped to make sure that these are legal rights.

3 Kodak has decided to make people redundant. Suggest ways in which it could have changed its business to keep its workers employed.

 **WORD BANK**

Redundant – when a job no longer exists, the worker who did that job is redundant – that is, not needed any more; this is not the same as being sacked

Redundancy benefit – the money that workers are paid by the business because their jobs no longer exist

Industrial disputes – arguments between groups of workers and employers

Industrial relations – the dealings between worker groups and employer groups

Trades unions – bodies set up by groups of workers to act for them

CBI – the Confederation of British Industry

Collective bargaining – when a group of people (like a trades union) negotiate to solve a problem

Strike action – when a person decides to refuse to work; also called 'withdrawing labour'

ACAS – this stands for the Advisory, Conciliation and Arbitration Service; it

- gives advice
- brings the two sides together (conciliates)
- makes decisions when the two sides cannot agree (arbitrates)

 REMEMBER THIS

It is in the interests of both employers and employees that industrial disputes do not happen. If they do happen, it is vital to solve them quickly. Most businesses solve disputes within the business. Often this is with the help and support of employer and employee organisations. Sometimes it is necessary to bring in outside bodies. The main body like this is ACAS.

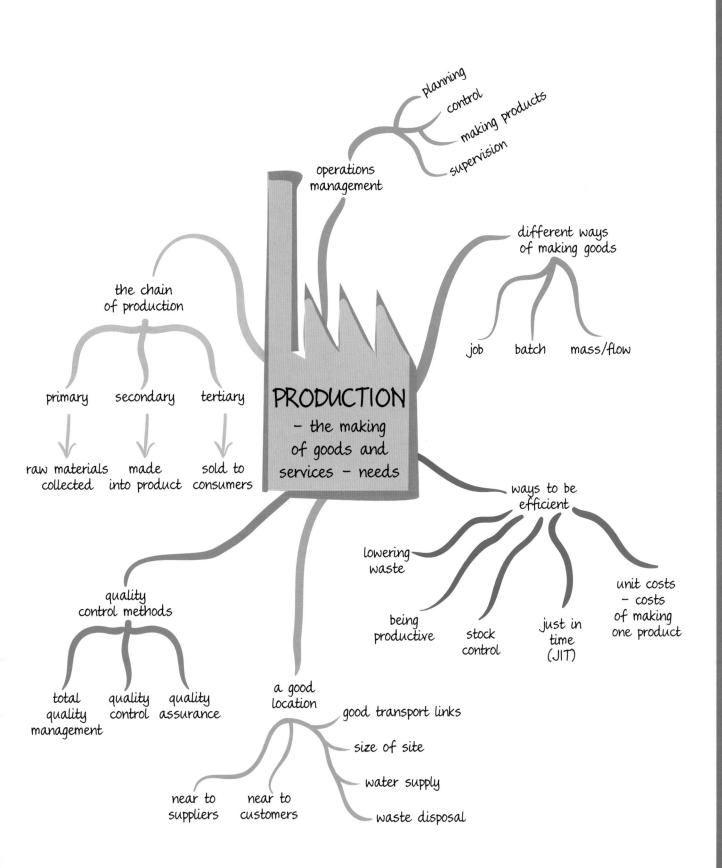

operations
management

planning
control
making products
supervision

different ways
of making goods

job   batch   mass/flow

the chain
of production

primary   secondary   tertiary

raw materials   made   sold to
collected   into product   consumers

PRODUCTION
– the making
of goods and
services – needs

ways to be
efficient

lowering
waste

being
productive   stock
control   just in
time
(JIT)   unit costs
– costs
of making
one product

quality
control methods

total
quality
management   quality
control   quality
assurance

a good
location

good transport links

size of site

water supply

near to   near to   waste disposal
suppliers   customers

Production

Unit 39 The chain of production

REVIEW THIS

As a product is created, it passes through several stages. These stages form a kind of chain, with each stage linked together. All products go through some chain of production before they reach the final customer. At each stage, a wide range of resources will be used, and there may be several businesses involved. Businesses will hope to add value as they make and sell the product.

READ THIS

When you next eat a bar of chocolate such as a Mars bar or a pack of bitesize chocolates such as Smarties, stop and think about all the resources that have gone into the product. At the heart, of course, is the cocoa bean grown on cocoa trees in Africa, Central and South America and parts of Asia. Other materials needed will include sugar, milk and flavourings, while large amounts of paper will be required for packaging. Chocolate manufacturers need large factories, complex machinery, large warehouses and fleets of lorries. Also, no bar of chocolate can be produced without the wide-ranging skills of all sorts of workers.

THE BASICS

Production is the process by which a good or service is created to meet the needs of customers. At each stage of the process, the product will have **value added**. The final value is achieved once the product is sold to a consumer. This can be shown with the following simplified example.

Coffee table production process

Stage	Input	Output	Value Added
Cut down trees	£0	£15,000	£15,000
Saw and trim wood	£15,000	£38,000	£23,000
Make coffee tables	£38,000	£65,000	£27,000
Total added value			£65,000

In this case, coffee tables have been sold to customers for a final value of £65,000. This has been created in three stages. It started when the trees were cut down and sold to a timber merchant for an added value of £15,000. The timber merchant saws the trees into various lengths and widths, and then sells them on to a coffee table manufacturer. This stage has £23,000 of added value. When the coffee table manufacturer turns the wood into finished tables and sells them direct to customers, this adds £27,000 value to the prepared wood. Add up the added value at each stage, and it comes to the £65,000 that the coffee tables sell for.

There are lots of ways to group the resources needed for any production. Some clues are given in the 'Read this' section. Land will be needed, perhaps to grow materials or to construct buildings. The buildings themselves are a major resource – shops, factories, warehouses or offices. Raw materials are a major resource in some industries, especially in food manufacturing. Other manufacturers will require huge quantities of parts and components – no car could be assembled without them, for example. Equipment is a major resource for virtually all businesses but items can vary greatly both in size and value.

No business can operate without workers giving both manual and mental effort. At the heart of all business is the entrepreneur. This person organises all the other resources and puts in money, hoping to make a profit but possibly risking losing their investment.

Chains of production

Every product has a chain of production with each stage linked to the next. There might be a different number of stages, but products will start at the `primary production` stage. This is where the raw material is extracted. From here, the raw material will enter the `secondary production` stage. This is where it is processed or manufactured into a finished product. Finally, the product will enter the `tertiary production` stage. The finished product will be distributed to businesses prepared to sell it to the final consumer. This stage includes all the commercial services such as banking and advertising, and the direct services of people like doctors and hairdressers.

WORD BANK

Value added – the difference between the value paid for the inputs used in production and the value of a business's output

Primary production – the first stage of the production process where raw materials are extracted, e.g. forestry, farming, mining and quarrying

Secondary production – at this stage of the production process raw materials are manufactured and processed into the final good

Tertiary production – this is the provision of all kinds of services, both to business and to the general public

DO THIS

Illustrate the chain of production for a bar of chocolate using the following stages.

Ripe cocoa pods are cut from the trees, broken open and the beans removed. The beans are allowed to ferment for up to six days and then dried. Manufacturers buy these beans and clean them. The shells are cracked open and then roasted. The beans are then ground to create a cocoa paste. Different varieties of cocoa paste are blended to create the desired flavour. Cocoa paste is then mixed with cocoa butter, sugar and milk to create a chocolate mixture. Stirring, heating and moulding then create the particular shape of chocolate bar. It is wrapped, placed in boxes and sent to the warehouse where it awaits distribution to wholesalers and retailers. Finally, it ends up in our hands, poised for that all-important bite!

REMEMBER THIS

Resources are needed for production to take place. Most products go through a chain of production, from the primary stage through a secondary stage to the tertiary stage before reaching the final customer. Value is added at each stage as the product is made.

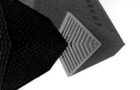

Production

Unit 40 The operations function

REVIEW THIS

The operations function is another name for a production department. Most firms only have a production department when they are involved in manufacturing or constructing a product. The main functions of the department are planning and controlling production. In smaller businesses, the production department may have extra roles such as purchasing materials and arranging storage. Every production department will be organised differently from those in other firms.

 READ THIS

Housebuilders are a good example of an organisation with a clear production department. There will be several sections of key workers: bricklayers, carpenters, roofers, plasterers, plumbers, electricians and installation fitters. A manager will be responsible for the whole building site, and will depend on supervisors to control the work of each section of workers. Each section will need materials and parts to arrive on time. They will also need to be given clear instructions, and will probably have to achieve targets.

THE BASICS

Once a product has been designed, its manufacture or assembly has to be planned carefully. The production department has many important decisions in this planning, like these listed.

- Which materials and parts will be needed and how much/many?

- How will the materials or parts be stored?

- What machinery, equipment and tools will be needed?

- How many workers will be required, and what range of skills and experience will they need to offer?

- What manufacturing method will be used?

- How will the product be packaged?

- How many units will be produced, and over what amount of time?

- How will production be controlled?

Production control stage

Once production plans have been completed, manufacturing can start. This is when the department must have controls in place. It needs to make sure that production takes place correctly, and that targets are met. At this production control stage, a number of important tasks will be required. Some of the main tasks are likely to be those listed below.

- **Equipment needs maintenance so that it does not break down and stop production. Faulty machines can easily produce large numbers of faulty products.**

- **Stocks of materials or parts need to be checked. If the firm runs out, production will probably stop. Too many stocks, however, could lead to waste and higher costs.**

- **Ways to measure the output of workers, machines and sections will need to be used to check on progress. The business needs to know if it is meeting production targets. The department may need to switch workers around if one section is slower than others.**

- **Quality checks need to take place to make sure that the finished item is up to standard and can be sold.**

In large manufacturing businesses, a production department may have several layers in its structure, and several specialist job titles. Broad job titles are likely to include engineers, manufacturing staff, storage staff, quality controllers and maintenance staff. The work of each of these titles will vary from firm to firm.

Example of a chain of command
A manufacturing section might be layered like this.

1 At the top there will be a manager in charge of a particular **production line**. This person will be responsible for the planning, making and controlling the output of one major product.

2 The manager will probably have at least one **production supervisor**. This person will be an experienced and highly skilled worker. The supervisor will check the work of all those working in the section. Problems will be reported to the manager, if necessary, and the supervisor will carry out the decisions of the manager.

3 At the bottom of this chain is the **production operative**. This person will make the products as part of a production team, and will be working to set targets. The operative will carry out instructions from the supervisor and will be talking to that person about any problems.

In the very largest firms, the purchase of materials and parts is carried out by a specialist purchasing department. This is run by a purchasing manager, together with purchasing assistants and buyers. A central purchasing department can often keep costs down because it can buy in bulk. If a firm is not large enough to have a separate purchasing department, the production department will usually be responsible for buying resources and parts.

DO THIS

Choose three items that you are carrying or wearing or that are in your classroom. Write a list of the materials and parts in each one. Explain how you think they have been made. Decide which you think will take the longest to produce and why.

WORD BANK

Production line – a complete section producing one type of good

Production supervisor – an experienced worker put in charge of other workers on the production line

Production operative – a person using machinery and actually responsible for making the good

REMEMBER THIS
The operations department is responsible for producing goods. In large businesses there may be several production lines in several factories. The department is likely to have several layers of people responsible for managing, controlling and making goods. In some firms, the department may also be responsible for purchasing materials and parts.

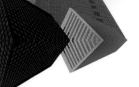

Unit 41 Manufacturing methods

REVIEW THIS

When a business has to decide how to produce its goods and services, it will probably have to carry out a great deal of research and development. Part of this research will be into the best method to make the product. The business will also investigate which strategies it can use to make the product efficiently.

READ THIS

FOOD SCARE CAUSED BY SUDAN 1

In February 2005, a major food scare hit the headlines in the UK. A dangerous dye, Sudan 1, had been used as one of the ingredients in over 450 food items on sale in major supermarkets. Each of these items was identified by its name and batch number. This was important as it narrowed down the problem foods to those that had used the dangerous dye. Only those items had to be recalled and destroyed. Customers, retailers and manufacturers could be confident that only those batches of those brands had been affected, thanks to the use of batch production.

THE BASICS

There are three main ways of manufacturing a product.

Job production

Job production means that a product is made individually from start to finish. Each product is likely to be different, and designed to meet a customer's personal specifications. Many services involve jobbing, while the range of products may vary from the very small to the very large. Road bridges, aeroplanes, house extensions, plumbing services, haircuts and jewellery are all good examples of job production. One advantage of this method is that the product is likely to reach a high quality. It certainly requires highly skilled workers, and this helps to motivate them. A final advantage is that each good is different in some way to all the others.

The major disadvantage is that jobbing can be quite expensive. The business has to use a lot of expensive, skilled labour, and it will find it difficult to speed up production.

Batch production

Batch production involves making groups of similar or identical items. In other words, the goods are made in batches. This means that once one batch is made, the machinery is stopped and settings are altered. The next batch can then be produced. Good examples of products made by batch production include bread, sweets, medicines, wallpaper and clothing.

This method helps to give more variety of goods, and some machinery can be used to produce more than one type of good. Unit costs are likely to be lower than they are under jobbing. Workers are still likely to be highly motivated, as a range of skills are usually needed and there is some variety.

The disadvantages will include storage costs and lost production time, resulting from having to stop and reset machinery.

Bread is made using the batch production method

Continuous flow

Flow production is sometimes called mass production because large numbers of goods are made. The machinery will rarely stop, with the product passing through a large number of specialised operations. This is often along some kind of conveyor belt. A good example is a car factory, with the basic car moving along as hundreds of items are added to it. This method also includes products made by a process. Breweries and petrol refineries are good examples of this.

The main advantage of this method is that large numbers of items can be produced at a low unit cost. Little production time is lost and each item should be of the same quality.

However, the disadvantages include the huge cost of machinery and the difficulty in changing the production line. Workers often need only a small range of skills and may feel that the job does not motivate them. For some consumers, the products may be too similar and give little choice. For the manufacturers, any breakdown can cause major problems.

The real world

In modern factories, many businesses use a combination of batch and flow production. For example, many pharmaceutical products are made in large numbers using flow methods, but they are likely to be made in batches. This allows the testing of the materials used, as well as the finished item. Each batch can then be given a special code to identify it and allow it to be traced in case of problems. This certainly helped in the case of the problems described earlier with the dye Sudan 1.

A special strategy used by many businesses, whether producing by job, batch or flow production, is **just-in-time**. The idea is that the business receives stocks of materials and parts just in time for them to be used in the production process. This cuts down on the costs of storage, and helps with its cash flow. Problems arise if there is any delay or if the stocks are faulty. This is why businesses using this technique must work closely with the companies supplying the stocks.

DO THIS

Try to find out which manufacturing methods are used to make the following products.

- Television sets
- Computers
- DIY electric drills
- Lorries
- Trains
- Tins of baked beans
- Chocolate bars

Explain why you think the businesses involved have chosen their methods.

WORD BANK

Job production – producing a single 'one-off' product or service to meet the individual requirements of a customer

Batch production – the production of a similar or identical good in batches, with the production stopped to allow for modifications before the next batch is made

Flow production – the manufacture of identical goods in large numbers on a continuous production line

Just-in-time – strategy involving the supply of stocks to the producer just in time for their use in the production process

REMEMBER THIS

There are three main methods of manufacturing goods: job, batch and flow. Each business has to decide which method best suits its particular products and the size of the business. Many modern businesses use a mixture of methods to manufacture goods and to provide services.

Unit 42 Location of industry

REVIEW THIS

When a business is planning to start a new operation, one of the most important decisions it has to make is where to locate its business. Whatever the business does, it will consider a number of factors. Ideally, the location will keep costs to a minimum, while helping to make as much revenue as possible. Sometimes, decisions will be influenced by outside bodies such as the government.

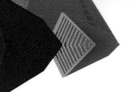

READ THIS

When Nissan wanted to build its first UK car manufacturing plant, it decided what it wanted from a location. It then looked at several sites around the UK. It wanted a large area of land, with plenty of room for expansion. It needed good transport links to bring in all the components and to send the finished cars to the markets, both in the UK and in Europe. Plenty of available labour with the right skills and attitude was a key factor. Finally, a site with some government financial assistance helped swing the decision in favour of Sunderland.

THE BASICS

There are a variety of factors that a business might have to consider when choosing the best location. Sometimes only a few factors will be really important to a business. Other businesses may have to consider and balance a mixture of location factors.

Geographical factors

For some businesses, geographical factors might be important. A business might need to be near a large supply of water. Others might need an area where waste can be stored safely. Businesses creating smell, dust or smoke might want the wind to blow in a particular direction for much of the time. A business might have to locate in a remote area because the product it makes is dangerous.

Cost of the site

The cost of the site is an important factor for most businesses. They will have to decide whether to rent or buy. The site might need to be levelled or drained. The business may have to decide whether to build on a **greenfield site** or a **brownfield site**.

Workforce

All businesses need to know whether there are enough workers with the right skills at their chosen location. They might need to know if there are training providers near by. Some businesses are attracted to areas of high unemployment, as wage rates may be lower. This would help to keep costs down.

Closeness to raw material or market

Costs are always an important consideration. If a product loses weight during the production process, a firm will have lower costs if it locates near the supply of the raw material. Steel and aluminium producers can both benefit from this. When a product gains weight during the production process, a firm will find its costs are reduced if it locates near to its market. Car manufacturers can benefit by locating near large centres of population.

Other factors

For some businesses, it will be important to find a site with room for expansion. For modern-day business, good transport and communications are vital. Locating near to motorways or to major ports and airports might be a key factor for some firms. In some cases, a business might need to locate near to firms that can provide services such as waste disposal, machinery repair and ICT support.

Some firms and industries are located in particular areas quite by chance. Many of our oldest businesses are located where they are because the original owner lived there. In some cases, the original reasons for locating in an area have disappeared. For example, the pottery industry was set up in the Midlands because that area had a supply of china clay. Now that the clay has run out the industry stays there because the area has other advantages. It has skilled labour and firms to provide all the necessary services.

Over the last 50 years, many industries have declined. Coal mining, iron and steel, shipbuilding and the cotton industries are all good examples of industries that have contracted, leading to high unemployment in many areas. Governments have tried to persuade new business to locate in those areas by offering various forms of help. Many of the areas of high unemployment have been labelled as **assisted areas**. Firms locating to or expanding in these areas might be able to receive a government grant towards their set-up costs. Sometimes factories are built ready for businesses to move into and rent at reduced rates. Lots of advice is usually available for businesses thinking of locating in an assisted area. Assistance with training is also often part of a package of help used to attract new business.

DO THIS

Think of some of the larger businesses in your local area. For each one, try to identify the possible factors influencing its location. Discuss your ideas in class. You might try writing to one of them and asking them to come in and talk about the factors influencing location.

WORD BANK

Greenfield site – a piece of land in the countryside, perhaps previously used for farming, which is developed and built on

Brownfield site – a site that was used for industry or housing, which is then redeveloped for new uses such as business and housing

Assisted area – an area or region with higher than average unemployment, given help to attract new or expanding businesses

REMEMBER THIS

When any business is deciding where to locate, there are many factors to consider. Most businesses try to find a site that keeps costs to a minimum while helping to maximise sales revenue. External help such as financial assistance, information, advice and training may persuade a business to choose one site over another.

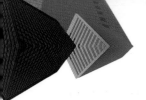

Production

Unit 43 Producing efficiently

REVIEW THIS

When a business has started to produce, it wishes to operate as efficiently as possible. This means trying to produce as many high-quality products as possible. It also means trying to keep costs as low as possible. Most businesses will set up ways to measure their efficiency. These can be checked to see how the business is performing and what needs to be done to improve.

READ THIS

It is quite difficult to measure efficiency when a service is being provided. For example, how does a bank know if it is being efficient? It could measure the time it takes for a bank clerk to deal with a customer. The problem with this is that the customer may have several transactions to make. The bank might try to identify the quietest times of the day and keep staffing levels down. This might lower the wage bill. One of the main ways in which a bank tries to measure efficiency is by checking the service offered to its customers. This can be done by using a 'mystery customer'. Another way is to carry out a survey of customer satisfaction.

THE BASICS

It is quite easy for a manufacturing business to measure its efficiency. Such firms measure the quantity of goods produced over a period of time.

This is known as measuring **productivity**. This may be done in a number of ways. A business could measure how many items are produced by a whole shift of workers. It could break this down by working out the average number of items made by each worker. Where much machinery is used, the business might decide to measure the output of each machine. No matter how the business measures its productivity, the higher the figure the more efficient it is.

Productivity may be reduced if a business has problems with its machines or with its workforce. To improve productivity, a business might introduce new machinery, or it might change the way it produces the goods. **Productivity deals** may be introduced, with workers being rewarded if they increase the output of goods.

Unit costs

As well as measuring productivity, most manufacturing businesses will use unit costs as an efficiency measure. This measures the cost of making a single good (unit). The simplest way is to divide total costs by the number of units made over a certain time period. For example:

$$\frac{\text{Total cost £50,000}}{\text{Output 20,000}} \quad = \quad \text{Unit cost of £2.50}$$

The lower the unit cost, the more efficient the business. Falling unit costs help a business to be more competitive, since they either help to increase profits or allow the business to lower prices if necessary. Obviously, rising unit costs are a problem for a business. A firm suffering this needs to find ways in which to reduce its costs or increase output.

Measuring waste

For some firms, measuring waste is an important way to see if they are being efficient. This is particularly so when a business creates a lot of waste. Wallpaper and clothing manufacturers are both likely to produce waste during the production process. Any waste material will cost the business money. Reducing waste will therefore help the business to be more efficient.

Stock levels

A business might look at its stock levels as a way of measuring and improving efficiency. A business needs enough stocks – raw materials, components, semi-finished goods, finished goods – to keep production flowing smoothly. Too few stocks of materials and parts will stop production. Too many, and the business may find that it is left with stock that perishes while it costs money to be stored.

Major changes and innovations

Sometimes a business may need to make a major change to the way it produces products. By carrying out a detailed work study, it might find both workers and machines standing idle for part of the time. This is not because a machine has broken down, nor is it because the workers are being lazy. It is because there is no work for them to do. By changing the way it operates, the business may be able to keep all machines and workers busy all of the time. This will help both productivity and unit costs.

Businesses that innovate are the ones most likely to improve efficiency. This might be achieved by introducing new machinery, new production processes, new products or new ways of operating. The business might have to carry out research into the ideas, and this will certainly cost money. Hopefully, though, the new innovations will pay for themselves through lower costs and higher revenue.

DO THIS

Create a table to summarise the measures of efficiency. You need to explain how each method is used, its advantages and disadvantages, plus suggestions of how efficiency might be improved.

WORD BANK

Productivity – measuring the quantity of goods produced over a period of time

Productivity deals – encouraging workers to increase output by offering them a pay deal linked to the number of goods produced

Innovation – introducing new products, new machinery, new production processes and new ways of operating

REMEMBER THIS

Efficient production means making the best use of all resources. This results in making the highest number of quality items at lowest unit cost. Measuring productivity, unit cost and waste helps to show whether a business is being efficient. Sometimes a business needs to completely change the way it operates in order to be more efficient. Stock control and introducing new technology can both help a business to improve efficiency.

Unit 44 Managing quality

REVIEW THIS

UK law states that any good produced by a business must be of the right quality for the customers to use. This makes it very important for businesses to set a standard and to keep to it when they produce each item. They might try to produce goods at an even higher standard than the one demanded by the law. They will certainly need to please their customers with the 'right' standard of quality.

READ THIS

For companies involved in making medicines, quality is the number one priority. The American-owned Pfizer group has a large factory at Morpeth in Northumberland. At this site, it produces a range of medicinal products, including Aldactone for helping heart disease and Celebrex for arthritis sufferers. In its state-of-the-art quality assurance building, it tests all the ingredients and all the batches of finished medicines. In the production buildings, staff are expected to carry out numerous quality checks as the drugs are made. This includes making regular checks on the settings of the machinery. Very sensitive weighing machines check that the finished packages are full, and special cameras can detect the smallest defects in the packaging of the blister packs.

THE BASICS

Every business has to decide what level of quality to aim for, whether it is producing a good or providing a service. It also has to decide how to achieve this. There are five key decisions for the business to make.

1 **What is the minimum level of quality required by the law?**

2 **What is the minimum level of quality required by customers?**

3 **How much higher than these minimum levels should the business aim?**

4 **Who is responsible for quality in the business?**

5 **How will the business ensure quality while keeping costs down?**

Quality controls

The traditional way to carry out **quality control** is to check the finished product. For example, finished bars of soap may be weighed, checked for shape, blemishes and smoothness, and a final check made on any logo stamped into the soap. With soap, any problem bars can be remixed so there is little waste. On the other hand, checking the quality of finished pottery items such as plates and mugs may create a lot of waste if they are faulty. If someone is employed to carry out quality-control checks, this also adds to the costs of the business.

Quality assurance

For pharmaceutical companies like Pfizer, it is important to check the quality of any ingredients used in producing their medicines. They also check quality at each stage of the manufacturing process, as well as at the end. This is known as **quality assurance**. It helps to ensure the quality of all products, but of course is likely to be expensive. The example of Pfizer shows that testers need to be employed, that a lot of equipment will be needed, and in this case a special building is required.

Statistical process control

Production workers at Pfizer's factory checking the settings of their machinery is an example of **statistical process control**. This contributes to good-quality products, but there is no guarantee that defective items are not made.

Total Quality Management

Many factories in a variety of industries now use the system of **Total Quality Management** (TQM). This system was created in the Japanese motor industry, and the basic ideas have spread around the world and into all sorts of manufacturing industries. Key features of TQM include the following.

- ○ **All workers in the business are expected to make quality their priority.**
- ○ **Every department is expected to be responsible for quality in some way.**
- ○ **Machinery is checked regularly and workers check the quality of the product as it leaves their workstation.**
- ○ **Teams of workers discuss how to improve quality.**
- ○ **All materials and parts are checked for quality.**
- ○ **Suppliers of parts and materials are expected to work closely with the business to help ensure top quality.**
- ○ **The needs and wants of customers always help to determine the minimum quality standards set by the business.**

The idea with this system is that 'quality is built in to the products', rather than being checked once production has taken place. The aim is to produce goods and services with no faults or problems. This will keep costs down and will help give the business a good reputation.

Kaizen

Another Japanese idea linked to quality is **Kaizen**. This means 'continuous improvement'. The idea is that a company and its workers are continuously trying to make the product and the production process better. It is thought that lots of small changes work best, rather than a few major changes.

DO THIS

Make a table to summarise the main features, advantages and disadvantages of the four methods of managing quality. Use the information in this unit to do this.

WORD BANK

Quality control – inspectors check the final products for defects

Quality assurance – quality is checked both before, during and at the end of the production process

Statistical process control – operators check their machines at regular intervals so that defects in products are minimised

Total Quality Management – everyone in the workplace is encouraged to be concerned about quality in everything they do

Kaizen – the company aims for continuous improvement through lots of small changes

REMEMBER THIS

All businesses have to make sure that their products are of a good enough quality for customers to use safely. Some businesses may decide to provide goods that are of a higher quality than the legal minimum. Businesses may use quality control checks, quality assurance or a Total Quality Management system to achieve the desired standards.

Unit 45 The marketing and sales function

REVIEW THIS

The marketing and sales function of a business is the area that finds out what the customer wants. It then has the job of making sure that the business has products to fill these wants. It also makes sure that the business promotes products in ways that will attract people to buy them.

Jobs in this area include:

- market researchers, who ask questions, observe market changes and collect market **data**

- analysts, who work out what the data collected mean

- designers, writers and artists, who create adverts

- buyers, who spend money on advertising and other promotions

- sales people.

Sometimes a change in a market will force a business into making changes.

READ THIS

In the summer of 2004, Kellogg's brought out a new version of its Frosties brand. This was in response to news that certain foods were being blamed for the growing problem of too many obese children. MPs put the food industry under pressure to reduce the amounts of sugar, salt and fat in products. Above all, they blamed those products that were promoted as being 'healthy' when they contained large amounts of salt and/or sugar.

The original Frosties cereal (which is still sold) contains 35 per cent sugar. In the new version, this has been reduced to 25 per cent. An adviser to the Consumers Association says, 'the new product still contains a lot of sugar. But today's announcement is a good sign that Kellogg's is

Continued ➔

starting to look at the high levels of sugar in some of its products.' Kellogg's is also changing the way it promotes products to children. A spokesman for marketing and sales at Kellogg's said that it will 'engage mums in the marketing of kids' products, and we'll be showing complete breakfasts in kids' ads'.
(*Source: Guardian* 13 July 2004)

THE BASICS

The way in which the marketing and sales area operates depends on the size and type of the business. In a small business, all the jobs may be carried out by a single person. This may be the owner in a sole trader business. It may be someone with more expert knowledge or training in a larger business. Some businesses will realise that they do not have enough expert knowledge to carry out the jobs. These may use a **marketing agency**. Agencies will produce an advertising campaign according to clients' wishes. This may include a complete image for a product. Kellogg's, for instance, is promoted through images to do with sport, healthy living and the family.

Businesses are also different in the way in which they approach the market. Some businesses create a new product and then try to persuade people to buy it. This applies to many electronic products like iPods and mobile phones. These are called **product orientated** businesses. These businesses will be trying to create a **gap in the market**. Many products are created for a certain time of year. Think about the race to produce a Christmas number-one single, for instance!

In other cases, a business makes and sells products in response to certain changes in the market. These businesses look at **market trends** and change products to fit with them. A business such as Kellogg's, for instance, may see a trend towards healthier eating. In response, it changes its product or the way it is promoted. Such businesses are said to be **market orientated**. These businesses will be looking for a gap in the market.

DO THIS

You are going to promote a product. Either use a product you have thought of and that you think the public will buy, or use an existing product that you know well. (Can you remember the different terms for these?) Draw an image of your product. Say which part of the market is your target. Around the image, write all the jobs that will be involved in promoting the product. Say what a person in each job would have to do to help promote your product.

LOOK AT THIS

Kellogg's promotes its products through images of sport, as it says that this will help persuade children to take more exercise. One major campaign is called 'earn your stripes'. This promotes football using Frosties 'mascot' Tony the Tiger.

1 List all of the marketing and sales people who would be involved in this campaign.

2 Describe the jobs that each would do.

3 Explain why Kellogg's uses these images and ideas to promote Frosties.

WORD BANK

Data – raw figures that have yet to be turned into information

Marketing agency – a business that specialises in marketing, used by other businesses to create marketing campaigns

Product orientated – businesses that are product orientated create a product and then promote it to a market

Gap in the market – a part of the market at which no product is targeted

Market trends – the way in which a market is moving; for instance, healthier living

Market orientated – businesses that are market orientated watch the market and create products to fit market trends

REMEMBER THIS

Marketing and sales is one of the functions carried out by a business. The jobs in this area involve finding out what customers want through market research and then making sure that the business provides this.

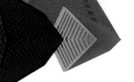
Unit 46 Market planning and customer profiles

REVIEW THIS

Remember that the marketing and sales area is in charge of finding out what customers want and then making sure that the business provides this. Part of the job of this area is to plan how a new product can be introduced, or how the market for an existing product can be changed. Sometimes the market plan is a response to a change in a market trend. Sometimes it is because those in the current target market have all been reached.

READ THIS

Businesses that issue credit cards in the UK appear to have reached all of their target market. In the past, a customer profile was built to show the type of person who would be offered a credit card. This was a person who was seen to be able to pay back money borrowed on the card. It was a person who had a good credit history and a good, steady income. In other words, it was someone who was in work and who paid off debts. Now all of this group seem to have not just one, but many cards. Many use one card to pay off others and do not want more new cards. This means that card companies are finding it hard to attract new custom. They have tried to persuade current credit card holders to take out new cards with special offers such as 0% interest, but this is not bringing in enough trade.

A report by accountancy firm PwC in the winter of 2004 predicted that, to gain new custom, the card companies will redraw customer profiles.

Continued →

The new profiles will aim cards at groups on low incomes or social benefits, and those with poor credit histories. Only by making these new groups its targets can the credit card issuers hope to keep high levels of growth. However, with the average debt on a card at almost £1,000, consumer groups are asking if it is fair for people on low incomes to be the new targets. (*Source*: adapted from *The Times*, 1 November 2004).

THE BASICS

Market planning involves finding out as much as possible about a market. A business will use its own internal information as well as information from other sources. It can also plan by using special tools to analyse its market. The business needs to know:

- **its own position in the market**
- **the competition in the market**
- **the part of the market it can target.**

There are many ways for a business to work out this information. Here are some examples.

It can use a **product map** to work out its position in the market. An example is shown below using some of the products made by Mars.

You can see from this that one direction in which Mars could expand would be luxury chocolate bars for children.

Another way to look at the position in the market is to carry out a **SWOT analysis**. This shows where the business stands with regard to the competition. SWOT stands for strengths, weaknesses, opportunities and threats, and is usually drawn up as a table, like the one shown for credit card issuers, below. Strengths and weaknesses are seen as internal – things the business can control. Opportunities and threats are seen as external – outside the control of the business, like interest rate changes.

Strengths	Weaknesses
Good product People need cards Good advertising and promotion Range of cards	Many customers can't pay Everyone targeted already has a credit card
Opportunities	**Threats**
New target market New types of card and promotions	New forms of cheap borrowing Warnings in the press about debt Many competitors Higher interest rates

To find the part of the market it can target, the business can create a **customer profile**. This is where the business creates an idea of its 'perfect' customer. The customer profile needed to be issued with a credit card used to be:

- good job and income
- keen to spend money
- uses well-known stores
- pays at least the minimum payment per month.

As mentioned above, this looks like it will now change to target a new type of customer on a lower income. When the card issuer has chosen the right target, it will then change the marketing mix (see Section 9) to make sure that it hits the target.

LOOK AT THIS

Look at the product map.

1 Choose a business with a wide range of products and draw up a product map for it.

2 Using your map, advise the business of way it should or could expand.

3 Explain why the business should expand in the direction that you have suggested.

DO THIS

Imagine you are opening a business in your local area.

1 Outline what your business will sell. What do you think your area needs? What do you think would attract customers?

2 Draw up a customer profile for the ideal customer for your business.

3 Explain why you have chosen this business and this customer profile.

REMEMBER THIS

Market planning involves finding out as much about your market as you can. This includes having an idea of who is the ideal customer for the business to target. The people in charge of marketing can then plan when, where and how to spend money to make sure that the product sells.

Unit 47 Market research

REVIEW THIS

Part of the job of the marketing and sales department or area in a business is to find out what the customer actually wants. In a small business the owner may do this. A business may also choose to use a specialist agency. The business can then go ahead and either:

- produce new products, or
- change existing products

so that they have the features that customers want. There are various ways in which a business can find out this information.

READ THIS

Nestlé Rowntree is the company that produces the Kit Kat chocolate bar. This is one of the most successful products ever. It has been a leader in the confectionery market for around 50 years. In the summer of 2003, Kit Kat was finally knocked off its top spot by arch-rival, Cadbury's Dairy Milk. In that year, Kit Kat's sales fell by 9 per cent. As a result, in the summer of 2004 the business planned a change to its advertising. For a long time, the successful slogan had been 'Have a break, have a Kit Kat'. This slogan is to be changed to 'Make the most of your break'. A spokesman for Nestlé says 'Our findings show that the workplace break is now less structured and formal. The new slogan is acknowledging

that the break is less formal but, you can still maximise your enjoyment with a Kit Kat.'

Nestlé has collected information about how consumers see the product. To find out what customers wanted, they asked them. It also has the market information showing the fall in Kit Kat sales. This showed that a change was needed. Nestlé then changed the way it promoted Kit Kat, to make it more attractive. Nestlé are acting on information collected through market research, planned and carried out by the marketing and sales area. (*Source: Independent*, 3 August 2004).

THE BASICS

Marketing and sales staff collect **data** that can be used to help the business to make marketing decisions. The business will need to know:

- **what sort of customers will buy the product**
- **how often they will buy it**
- **how much they are willing to pay**
- **what attracts them to buy the product**

Once they have found this information, they can then use marketing and advertising to make the product more attractive to buyers.

There are a number of ways of finding out what customers want. The two main types of research are desk research and field research.

Desk research is when someone else has already collected the data used. This data may be printed or on the internet. Because it has been collected before, desk research is also called secondary research. There are good and bad points to desk research.

- **On the good side, there is a lot of it (especially on the internet), most of it is readily available and much of it is free.**

- On the bad side, the research may not be exactly what a business needs, may be old or out of date and, in some cases, may be expensive to buy.

Field research is when the data is collected first-hand. Because it has not been collected before, field research is also called primary research. The most common ways to carry out field research are interviews, questionnaires, surveys, observation and testing. There are good and bad points to field research.

- On the good side, a business can plan to collect exactly the data it wants – asking specially designed questions of specially chosen groups of people.

- On the bad side, the research may take a long time to carry out, may be expensive, and it may be hard to find the right group of people to ask.

LOOK AT THIS

FOUR CYCLE ENGINE LUBRICANT

DOUBLE YOUR WARRANTY

Interlube International, Inc. will extend your warranty period on **internal engine** parts to twice that offered by the Engine Manufacturer.

HOW TO QUALIFY:

1. Make sure your new unit has been initially filled with **Opti-4** Four Cycle Lubricant and the engine sticker is attached.

2. Purchase a 6 pack or 2-1 gallon jugs of **Opti-4** Four Cycle Lubricant for top up and oil changes. Equipment and oil must be purchased at the same time and same location.

3. Use **Opti-4** Four Cycle Lubricant exclusively during entire Warranty period.

Name: _____

Address: _____

City: _____ State/Zip: _____

Equipment Brand: _____

Engine Brand: _____

Model Number: _____ Serial Number: _____

Place of Purchase: _____

Date Purchased: _____ Commercial or Casual Use: _____

Length of Original Warranty: _____

RETURN THIS COPY TO INTERLUBE

1226144

PRINTED IN CANADA

Look at this guarantee card. The business is collecting information about the product.

1 Outline three other ways by which the business could collect data.

2 Explain how the business is likely to use the data collected.

3 Explain the difference between data and information.

DO THIS

You could carry out a survey in your own class. Imagine that you are launching a new product. This needs to be a product that someone your age would buy. First decide on the information that you will need. Then write ten questions that you can ask. (Do not waste time asking questions that you already know the answers to – like 'Are you male or female?' or 'How old are you?') Try the questions on at least ten people. Look at the answers and then turn the data into information. What conclusions can you reach? How useful do you think such surveys are?

WORD BANK

Data – raw figures, comments and observations that have not been turned into something meaningful; when they have been turned into something useful, this is called information

Desk research – finding data from sources that have already been published; this is also called secondary research

Field research – finding data from original, first-hand sources; this is also called primary data

REMEMBER THIS

Market research is carried out to discover what it is that the customer actually wants and will pay for. It involves the collection of data from customers and people who may become customers. This data can then be turned into information that is useful to the business.

Unit 48 Customer service

Good food makes happy customers!

REVIEW THIS

Market research uses a number of ways to find out what customers actually want and how well a product is doing in the market. Field research is used to ask questions to customers directly, to see if the business is meeting their needs. Desk research is used to find information that has been collected by someone else and published. Businesses will not just want information about customers. They will also want information about the competition. Observation and desk research can be used to find out what is happening in the rest of the market.

Some of the research may be used to see if the customers who use the business are happy with it.

READ THIS

What any business wants is a happy customer. Happy customers are satisfied with what they have bought. They are also happy with the way that it was sold to them. A happy customer is one who will come back again, and who may well recommend the business to friends. They have the **customer loyalty** that the business needs. Businesses can succeed or fail because of a good or bad reputation. **Word-of-mouth** is very important to many businesses. But people are much more likely to tell others about bad experiences than good ones. It is said that a person will tell three others about a

Continued →

good meal out, but will tell twelve others about a bad one!

Food critics go out to review restaurants. The review, if it is good, can lead to a better reputation and increased trade. If it is bad, it can lead to reduced trade for the business. One restaurant critic recently wrote about the service at a well-known fish and chip shop. Writing about the staff he said, 'Their "happy to help" badges contrasted sharply with their "don't dare ask me" expressions, and although they displayed a huge sign reading "We don't have comment cards, but it is our pledge to listen", they ignored my enquiries.'

The review was published in a national newspaper. It describes the sort of customer service that could destroy a business. (*Source: Guardian*, November 2004).

THE BASICS

Good customer service helps to attract and keep customers. This is important to the success of a business. Different businesses will offer different types of customer service according to the type of goods or services they sell.

- **Providing information** – this could be given on the product itself, or by staff. Many products need clear labels so that customers can use them safely. In other cases, packaging is important, to protect or display the product. Information could also be in catalogues or leaflets or **point-of-sale material**. Staff should also be trained to give information.

- **Giving advice** – many businesses give free advice with products. This might be about the best way to use the product, or the safest way, or other advice. Customers expect specialist businesses to be able to give specialist advice. So a carpet store, for instance, should be able to advise on the best way to clean a carpet.

- Providing ways to pay – businesses need to make paying as easy as they can. They may let customers pay in a number of different ways. These could include cash, cheques or cards. They may provide ways to spread the cost, by offering **credit facilities**, or ways to **pay in instalments**.

- After-sales service – staff need to be able to deal with the service that customers may want after they have bought a product. This could include a delivery service, dealing with complaints or dealing with exchanges. It could also involve repairs and refunds.

Do not forget that good customer service applies to both goods and services. You would soon complain if your hair was not cut properly!

LOOK AT THIS

Look at the cards shown in the picture.

1 Describe what sort of cards these are, and how they are used.

2 Explain how these cards can benefit (a) customers; (b) the business.

3 Explain other ways that a business could try to persuade customers to come back again.

 **DO THIS**

Work with a partner. Choose two businesses that provide different products. For example, a car repair garage compared with a restaurant.

1 Each of you should write down the types of customer service that you would expect from one business. Then swap your lists to see if you agree.

2 With the whole class, list all the types of customer service.

3 Put the types in order of importance to (a) the business; (b) the customer.

Give reasons for your choices.

 **WORD BANK**

Customer loyalty – loyal customers will return to the business and use it again

Word-of-mouth – people saying good or bad things about a business; it is very important (and free)

Point-of-sale material – information that is displayed at the 'point of sale' – that is, where the customer actually pays for the product

Credit facilities – allowing customers to borrow money or goods and pay for them over a period of time

Pay in instalments – paying part of a debt at regular intervals – once a month, say

 REMEMBER THIS

Good customer service is vital to the success of a business. There are four main types of customer service. Businesses should be able to provide:

information; advice; different and convenient ways to pay; after-sales service.

If businesses can keep customers happy, then customers will be loyal to them. This means that customer are also likely to recommend them to friends.

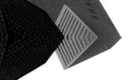

Unit 49 Measuring customer satisfaction

REVIEW THIS

One of the main aims of a business must be to keep its customers happy. They also need to be kept loyal, so that they come back and use the business again. Businesses need to collect as many details about customers as they can. This is so they know how to please them. Businesses give good customer service by giving information and advice. They also provide ways to pay and after-sales service. To see how effective these are, they need to try to measure customer satisfaction.

READ THIS

No young person wants to be behind the times. Everyone wants to be up to date. Providing the latest ringtones to people is an example of a market that is growing quickly.

Where do you, or your friends, buy your ringtones from? Chances are that, whether you know it or not, they are being supplied by Monstermob. This company made a deal with digital music business Wippit to supply it with ringtones. Wippit holds the rights to artists such as Christina Aguilera, Jamelia, Franz Ferdinand, Robbie Williams, Coldplay, David Bowie and Dido. It has over 100,000 downloads in stock. Customers can pay as little as 29p each for them. This keeps one section of the market happy. Or for £60 a year you can sign up for access to a huge and changing selection of

Continued →

tones. This keeps a further part of the market happy.

Monstermob has made the deal to make sure that it keeps its customers. Only by making the top tunes available will it keep its **market share**. It is also looking to the future. Mobile handsets now act as cameras, videos and mp3 players. More and more, they can network with other technology such as laptops and digital music players. Monstermob wants to be a leading player in the market. To do this it needs to keep its customers happy both now and in the future. (*Source*: *Yorkshire Post*, 16 November 2004).

THE BASICS

Most products carry a 'customer satisfaction guarantee' that says that you can return the product if you are not happy with it. This is the very least that people expect. Businesses may also measure satisfaction by seeing how many products are returned. **Customer satisfaction** means keeping customers happy. If they are happy, they will come back and buy from the business again. They will be loyal to the business. They will tell friends about the good points of the business. Even if a rival charges higher prices, customers will still come back if they think they are getting good service. So one way in which businesses can measure customer satisfaction is by the success of the business.

Some businesses set certain targets for good service; for instance, that the phone will always be answered quickly and politely, or that questions will always be answered in a set time. Businesses can use other ways to measure whether customers are happy; for instance, how often customers come back to buy again. They can check this if a customer uses the same card to pay or the same phone to place an order. They can ask customers what they think about the service. They may do this through surveys when they approach customers and ask them questions. They may do it by putting questions on order forms or running competitions. They may also measure satisfaction by the number of complaints received.

LOOK AT THIS

Usually the very least that a business will do is to provide a refund if a customer is not happy with what they have bought. It does not have to do this, but most will. The number of returns is just one of the ways to measure customer satisfaction. Make a list of all the other ways that a business can use.

DO THIS

Which services can you receive through your mobile phone? Which services can other people in your class or group get?

1 Make a list to include all of the services.

2 Suggest why your mobile phone company supplies such a range of services.

3 Explain which methods your mobile phone company could use to find out if you are a happy customer.

WORD BANK

Market share – the amount of the market that a business has; this is usually measured as a percentage

Customer satisfaction – making sure that customers are happy

REMEMBER THIS

Businesses rely on customers being loyal. They will only be loyal if they are kept happy. A happy customer will come back and buy from the business again. The sort of questions businesses use to see if they are keeping customers happy are:

○ Did they come back and buy again?

○ If they did, why? If they didn't, why not?

○ Did they tell a friend about us?

○ How many products have been returned?

○ How many complaints have we had?

○ How well were they solved?

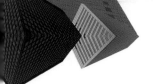
Unit 50 Consumer protection

REVIEW THIS

If a product seems to be a good one, people will buy it. This is especially true if it is at the right price. If it is promoted well and widely available, they will also buy. A good marketing mix can be enough to persuade people to buy a product. But what if the product is not as good as it is made out to be? What if it does not do the job that it is supposed to do? Would a bottle opener that did not open bottles be any good? Even worse, what if it is not safe? Luckily, people are protected against poor products, false claims and bad advertisements.

READ THIS

The law protects consumers in many ways. There are also some organisations that do not lay down the law, but that draw up 'codes of practice', or rules, for certain types of business. The Advertising Standards Authority is the body that checks whether or not adverts are fair. Sometimes it steps in to stop adverts if there are complaints. Sometimes it sets out rules or guidelines for advertisers.

In autumn 2004, it changed the rules on the ways in which alcohol is advertised. It decided that some adverts for drink targeted young people. They were aimed at teenagers who were not old enough to drink. The adverts also gave people the idea that alcohol would make them better liked or more attractive to the opposite sex. The new rules make it harder for drinks makers to promote brands to young people. They

also stop advertisers from making claims that alcohol can make you more attractive or sexy.

Under the new rules, adverts must not 'strongly appeal to under 18s by ... being associated with youth culture'. Drinkers shown in the adverts must also be obviously 25 or over. Drinks must be seen to be handled and served in a proper way. So a recent advert for Bacardi rum where ex-footballer Vinnie Jones sprays the drink around the bar will no longer be allowed. The new rules also ban adverts that link alcohol with 'daring, toughness ... or unruly, irresponsible or anti-social behaviour'. The rules are made to protect young people who might be influenced by the adverts.

THE BASICS

Any person who buys a good or service is a customer. Any person who uses a good or service is a **consumer**. This is a bigger group than just customers. It includes people who may not have bought things, but who are users, such as children and babies. You are a consumer. So you are protected by law. The least you should expect from a good is that it does what it is supposed to do. In other words, that it works as described. It should also work safely. The same is true if it is a service that you are using. The service should be carried out properly and safely, and within a reasonable time limit.

The law also says that you must act sensibly as a consumer. The legal phrase used is 'let the buyer beware'. (You will sometimes see this given in its Latin form of **caveat emptor**.) This means that you should check goods before you buy them and not buy any products with obvious faults. The main consumer protection **acts** concern quality, safety, fairness and accurate information.

Continued →

- **Quality.** This means 'fit for purpose' – the product should do what it is meant to do.

- **Safety.** Products must be safe. There should be warnings of possible harmful effects.

- **Fairness.** Consumers should receive what they paid for. Sale prices should be genuine. When buying on credit, it must be clear what the charges will be.

- **Accuracy.** Weights and measures must be truthful. Ingredients must be shown on products. Information about what a product can do or how it may be used should be correct.

LOOK AT THIS

1 Look at the information printed on the back of this product. Which of it is:

- advice to the consumer
- warning the consumer
- just advertising?

2 Say which of the information must legally be given.

3 Explain which information is, in your opinion, most important to the consumer. Give reasons for your answer.

DO THIS

You are a (teenage) consumer. Other people draw up the rules that protect you from bad sellers and bad adverts. With a partner, draw up your own set of rules that you think should be applied to selling and advertising as far as teenagers are concerned.

Explain why some groups of people (including teenagers) may need to be protected from advertising. Outline which groups you think these are. Explain whether you agree with the protection that is given.

WORD BANK

Consumer – any person who uses a good or service

Caveat emptor – the Latin phrase that means 'let the buyer beware', and which tells consumers that they have a responsibility to act sensibly when buying

Acts – short for acts of parliament, which the government uses to make laws

REMEMBER THIS

You are a consumer. There are laws to protect you when you are buying or using products. You are protected from unfair dealing by sellers. You are given information about the products you buy, such as the ingredients in food, or the way to operate a machine, or the correct way or length of time to store something. When you buy on credit, you will be given clear information about the costs to you. If you ever feel like you have been cheated in any way, you can return the product and receive a refund. You are also protected from bad advice and bad adverts.

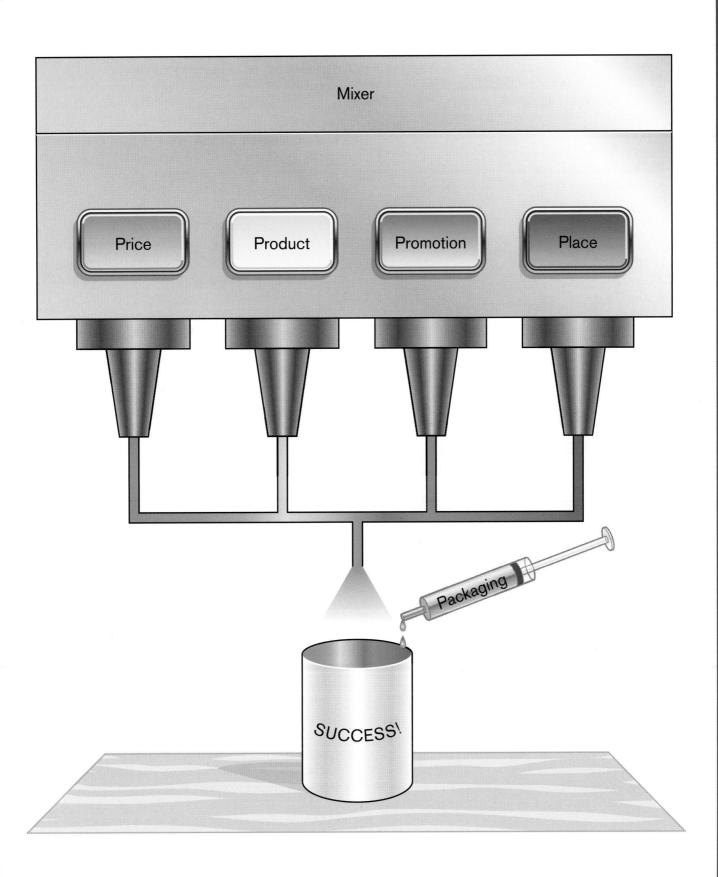

Unit 51 Product

REVIEW THIS

A business needs to have a good or service to offer for sale. This is called the **product**. It is just one part of the marketing mix. A business needs the right product – something that people want to buy. It needs to be able to set the price at a level that people will pay. With the right product and price, the business is halfway to a successful marketing mix. It can then decide how to promote the product and where to sell it. Without a product, there would be no business, so it is perhaps true to say that it is the most vital part of the mix.

READ THIS

Hornby is a business whose product is toys. It has been making and selling toys for over 50 years. It is well known throughout the world as a maker of model train sets. It also sells model racing cars and owns the Scalextric brand. Scalextric cars are electronically controlled cars that race on a track. But model trains and racing car games are things that today's buyers may think of as old-fashioned. So Hornby is always trying to improve on what it sells. It could improve its product by making it better, or it could improve its product range by selling other toys that its customers might want.

The company decided to improve its product by introducing a digital track system. This means that both trains and cars stay on the track better.

Continued →

For the model train buyer this means that up to 50 trains can be run at any time on one track layout. For Scalextric fans it means that they can now race cars against each other properly as they can now overtake. Hornby has also improved its product range by bringing out new cars to run on the digital track. These include Ferraris and Batmobiles. Hornby wants to break out of its niche market and into the mass toy market. To help it to do this, it has a licence from the *Batman Begins* film to make and sell the Batmobile. Signs of the success of Hornby could be seen in increased sales and increased profits.

THE BASICS

The product is the good or service a business offers for sale. Some businesses just sell one product; for instance, plumbers or taxi drivers sell their services. Some will sell a narrow **range of products** in a particular area, as with Hornby selling toys. Others will sell a wide range of products. Many of these are well-known names such as Cadbury's, Nestlé and Microsoft. Others, like Unilever, may not be as well known as they tend not to use their company name as a brand. Unilever is known for its soap products like Persil and Dreft. It also makes many other products, including beauty aids, margarine and scent. Each brand is aimed at just one part of the market.

The business needs to make each product different from the competition. This is called **product differentiation**. One way to do this is for each product to have its own brand name. Other ways of making products unique include changes to quality, flavour, size, design or other features. A common way to make products stand out is to package them in different ways. Even though the product inside might be the same, people are willing to pay more for a branded product in a fancy box than for the cheaply packaged alternative.

Product development is used when a product is being launched on to the market, or when sales have started to fall. Hornby developed trains, track and control systems when it first started selling model trains. It has further developed its product by using new technology.

The most important thing about a product is its **quality**. This does not mean whether it is cheap or not, but whether it does what it is meant to do.

Unit 52 Product life cycles

REVIEW THIS

The product is the most important part of the marketing mix. It is the good or service that a business offers for sale. Each product will have its own life cycle. It will be 'born', it will 'grow old' and, eventually, it will 'die'. Businesses will try to keep the product going for as long as it is making a profit. There will be special links with other parts of the marketing mix at each stage. All of the parts of the marketing mix will be important in making the life of the product as long as possible.

READ THIS

Video recorders were first brought out in 1978. Until then it was only possible to watch a programme at the time that it was broadcast. Video recorders changed the viewing patterns for television. The first one aimed at the home market was priced at £798.75 (around £3,500 in today's prices). Two systems were launched, but VHS quickly defeated the slower Betamax system.

After a life of just over 25 years, the death of the video recorder was announced in 2004. High-street retailer Dixons announced that it would no longer be stocking video recorders. It said that DVD players were outselling videos by more than 40 to 1.

When video recorders were launched the price was a special high price because they were new. (Unit 53 explains more about this type of price 'skimming'.) The market then grew as more and

Continued →

more people bought them. Eventually almost everyone had a video so sales began to fall. Even though prices were lowered and new features added, sales still fell. Finally, Dixons decided to stop selling video recorders. At the same time, the government announced a fall in some crime figures. The number of house burglaries had fallen because the robbers could no longer sell the goods they had stolen. This was because, in the case of many of the goods, every household already had one.

THE BASICS

Product life cycles show the way in which sales of a product change over time. This can be shown on a graph. Most products do well when they are first launched. They then have steady growth in sales. If the product is a success, other businesses will start selling it. There may come a point when the market is 'full'. In other words, everyone has got one. This is called **market saturation**. At this point, the business will find it has sold as many as it can, so sales start to fall. Finally, the product is no longer wanted. At this point it is taken off the market.

Businesses will try to make the life cycle longer. They do this by changing or adding to a product. These changes are called **product extension strategies**. If it works, this is called an **extended life cycle**. Sometimes the cycle happens over a short period of time, perhaps only a few weeks. This is called an **explosive life cycle**. Sometimes it happens over a long period of time, perhaps as long as 50 or 60 years. The cycle for VHS recorders was around 25 years.

The product life cycle has five stages (see the table on the opposite page).

The longer a product can be kept on the market, with only small changes every so often, the better it is for the business. It does not have to bother spending money on new machines or equipment, or on new products. Some products are such a success that businesses can rely on them to keep selling. They then use the money made from them to develop new products.

	Stage	Description
1	Launch	When the product is first brought out
2	Growth	Sales grow as the product is promoted and becomes well known
3	Maturity	Sales slow down. Most people have one, and now there are competitor products
4	Saturation	Sales go down. Everybody has one already! There are lots of competitor products. These may be cheaper and better
5	Decline	Sales fall quickly. The product is withdrawn from the market

LOOK AT THIS

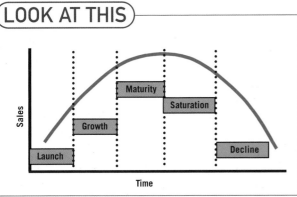

You should be able to see how different parts of the marketing mix are used at the various stages of the life cycle. For instance, when the product is launched, it may need a lot of promotion. When it is starting to fail, it may need to be sold at a low price.

1 Copy out the graph. Add a definition for each part of the life cycle.

2 (a) For each stage, give the type of price that might be charged.

   (b) For each stage, give the type of promotion that might be used.

3 Explain why you think the price and promotion you have chosen would be used.

DO THIS

Write down a product that you think has had an explosive life cycle. Write down a product that you think has had an extended life cycle. Write down a product that is now part of a saturated market. Share your ideas with a group and draw up a three-column list of the products. Then share the list with the rest of your class. How many different products can you name? Do you all agree on them?

WORD BANK

Product life cycle – the normal five stages that a product's sales pass through

Market saturation – when there are too many products and not enough people wanting them, usually because everybody already owns one

Product extension strategies – changes used by a business to make the life of a product longer

Extended life cycle – making the life cycle longer by making changes to the product or the way it is sold

Explosive life cycle – a short product life cycle with fast growth and fast decline

REMEMBER THIS

The product life cycle shows the stages of sales that a product goes through. It is a vital tool to help businesses plan. Product extension strategies can be used to make a product last longer in the market. To make sure of success, a business must ensure that the other parts of the marketing mix are right.

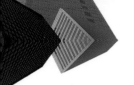

Unit 53 Price

REVIEW THIS

For a product to sell, it has to be something that buyers want. It also has to be at the right price. To make people aware that the product exists, sellers will need to advertise it. This can also be used to help persuade people to buy the product. The product also has to be available at places where people who want to buy it can find it. A business needs to have the correct combination of these four things – product, price, promotion and place. It is like having the right recipe for success. The mixture is called the marketing mix.

READ THIS

JD Wetherspoon is a business that runs a chain of high-street pubs. Towards the end of 2004, it warned that its sales were falling. It said that it was making lower profits than expected. This is because it had been forced to cut prices to keep its customers. In recent years, there have been many businesses that have tried to set up and survive as high-street pubs. Some have been sold off, as their owners could no longer see them making a profit. These include Yates Group and Eldridge Pope. Others such as Regent Inns have issued many warnings about lower profits.

The problem in the trade has been that there are just too many businesses competing for a smaller and smaller part of the market. Pubs have been in what is called a 'price war'. This means that

they keep making prices lower and lower to try to attract custom. Because of this their profits also become lower and lower. Those businesses that find they cannot compete end up leaving the market. They may just decide not to trade in that market any more and sell up. They may be forced out of business. (*Source: Independent*, 2 October 2004)

THE BASICS

Imagine you were setting up in business selling pens. You have found a supplier who will sell you the pens at 10p each. But how much will you sell them for? This is the question that all businesses must ask themselves. Your first price decision is going to be to sell the pen at more than you paid for it. You might think that selling a pen for 11p would be fine. But are you sure that you have covered all your costs? What about the time and effort spent in getting the pens? What about the costs of selling them – say a stall or shop? What about your own reward? To make sure that you are making a profit, the selling price must cover all of these things. The usual way to work it out is called **cost plus pricing**.

Price = unit cost + overheads + mark-up

- **Unit cost** is the cost to buy each pen. In our case, this is 10p.
- **Overheads** refer to the other costs that must be paid before the pen is sold.
- **Mark-up** refers to the extra (profit) that you want to make for yourself.

So you may find that you have to charge much more than you thought! The price you charge must be one that people will pay. They will compare your price with those of other businesses selling pens and use the one they feel will give them value for money. You can try to add value and persuade people to buy by using other parts of the marketing mix.

Continued ➔

LOOK AT THIS

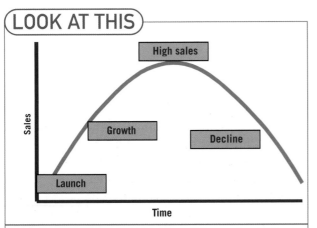

Products often go through a life cycle. This starts with the launch of the product. It then sells well. In time, sales will fall. Finally it dies off. (There are more details on this in Unit 52.) This is a simple life cycle. Copy the diagram and mark on it what sort of price you think would be charged at each stage. Explain why you think this.

DO THIS

Sometimes a business may charge a price which means it is not making a profit. JD Wetherspoon could make some drinks much cheaper in order to attract people into its pubs. It might even charge less than the cost of the drink. This is called a loss leader. Making a loss on a product like this draws people into the pub, where they might spend on other products, on which JD Wetherspoon *does* make a profit. There are other special types of pricing.

1 Look at the table and match the definition

Cost plus pricing	Price set where a profit is not made
Loss leaders	Sales and special offers
Penetration price	Prices set to cover costs
Promotional pricing	Low price charged to gain a share of a market

with the price.

2 Suggest other special types of pricing that a business could use.

3 Explain what is meant by 'value for money'. How does this affect pricing?

WORD BANK

Cost plus pricing – working out a price that covers costs and makes a profit

Unit cost – the cost to buy or make each item, also called variable cost

Overheads – other costs that must be paid, also called fixed costs

Mark-up – the extra added on to costs to make a profit

REMEMBER THIS

In order to sell products, businesses have to achieve the correct marketing mix. This is the mix of price, product, promotion and distribution. Prices have to be set at a level that covers costs. They will usually be set to also make a profit. Businesses also use special types of price. Some of these will be low, some high, but all are designed to make the business a success. No business will succeed if customers do not buy from it. So prices have to be at a level that gives value for money. Price is just one way in which businesses compete with each other.

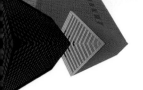

Unit 54 Promotion

REVIEW THIS

Two parts of the marketing mix are the product and price. The success of a product depends on getting these right. But the success of a product also depends on it being well known. People will not buy a product if they do not know it exists! Promotion is about letting people know what products are on sale. Promotion is vital when a product is launched. It will also be used to grow sales and extend the life of a product.

READ THIS

The success of a promotion is often about getting the time and place right. Many products are launched in the run-up to Christmas. Among these will be new toys, new games and new films. Some will be promoted well enough to be a success. Others may never really catch on.

To film-makers, a Christmas hit is worth a lot of money. The major film aimed at viewers for Christmas 2004 was Pixar's *The Incredibles*. This is a cartoon movie but that did not stop the film-makers, from using real people to promote it. The launch took place with an event in London. The event was designed to gain good publicity for the film. Regent Street was closed to traffic while a free concert was staged. The final band to play was the teen boy band Busted. This would have been enough to attract many of the age group at which the film is aimed. At the end

Continued →

of the concert, Busted turned on the Regent Street Christmas lights. The lights themselves were designed to promote the film, showing characters that feature in it. Further publicity was gained by inviting a line-up of celebrities who were interviewed before the big 'switch on'. They included Samuel L Jackson, the American actor who provides the voice for the lead character. To strengthen the theme, various 'incredible' Olympic athletes were also introduced to the crowd. Of course, the whole event was reported on the television news and in the newspapers. This gave Pixar even more free publicity.

THE BASICS

There are two parts to **promotion**. Businesses have to tell consumers that a product exists – so promotion is about information. They also need to try to make consumers buy the product – so promotion is also about persuasion. The main parts of promotion are **advertising** and **public relations**. Advertising is promotion that is paid for. Public relations promotes a product indirectly.

Advertising may just give information, but it is more likely to try to persuade at the same time. So adverts always have a message. The means by which adverts pass on these messages are called the **media**. Broadcast media include radio, television and movies. The most powerful of these is television, and it is also the most expensive. Printed media include newspapers, magazines, posters, leaflets and direct mail. Sometimes the message is spread as widely as possible by using posters or television. Sometimes it is aimed at a target market by using **direct mail**. Businesses can even use email to target people.

Public relations (or PR) is used to promote the image of the product without directly paying for advertising. The Busted event on Regent Street was a free concert. The event did its job in attracting people. It was also shown on television and written about in the papers. Although it will have cost the business to stage the concert, the publicity that came from it would have cost a lot more had it had to pay for it directly. PR also includes sponsorship. This helps a business to keep its name known. Think about the sponsors of your local football club or sports stadium, for instance.

LOOK AT THIS

The **Guardian**

FreeCompactDisc

**PAUL WELLER
ALL ALONG THE WATCHTOWER**
(Dylan)
Produced by Ian 'Stan' Kybert and Paul Weller
Published by B.Feldman & Co Ltd
© 2004 Solid Bond Productions
Licensed to V2 Music Ltd
Taken from the album 'Studio 150'

**SONS AND DAUGHTERS
BROKEN BONES**
(Sons and Daughters)
Produced by Sons And Daughters
Published Copyright Control
© 2004 Domino Recording Co Ltd
Taken from the album 'Love The Cup'

**THE DELGADOS
I FOUGHT THE ANGELS**
(The Delgados)
Produced by Tony Doogan and The Delgados
Published by Chrysalis Music
© 2004 Chemikal Underground Ltd
Taken from the album 'Universal Audio'

**NICK CAVE AND THE BAD SEEDS
THERE SHE GOES, MY BEAUTIFUL WORLD**
(Cave)
Produced by Nick Launay and Nick Cave and
The Bad Seeds
Published by Mute Song Ltd
© 2004 Mute Records Ltd
Taken from the album 'Abattoir Blues/The Lyre Of Orpheus'

**MULL HISTORICAL SOCIETY
CASANOVA AT THE WEEKEND**
(MacIntyre)
Produced by Colin MacIntyre
Published by Warner/Chappell Music Ltd
© 2004 B-Unique Records
Taken from the album 'This Is Hope'

**TRASHCAN SINATRAS
WEIGHTLIFTING**
(Trashcan Sinatras)
Produced by Trashcan Sinatras
Published by Rights Worldwide Ltd c/o Faber Music Ltd
© 2004 Picnic Records
Taken from the album 'Weightlifting'

This CD is free with the Guardian newspaper. For promotional purposes only. Not for broadcast or resale. Not to be sold separately. All rights of the producer and of the owner of the recorded works reserved. Unauthorized copying, public performance, broadcasting, hiring or rental of the recording is prohibited

The producers of this CD have paid the composers and the publishers for the use of their music

Businesses are always trying to think of new ways to promote products. It has now become so cheap to make a CD that some papers give them away to promote LPs. The CD shown was given away with the *Guardian*. It promotes six LPs by letting readers listen to a track from each. List all the possible ways that could be used to promote a film or CD.

DO THIS

Promotion has to be aimed at the right part of the market to be a success. *The Incredibles* film is aimed at young people. Busted is a boy band that has young people as fans. So the two can be used together for promotion.

With a partner, think of five recent films. For each one, suggest the target market, and suggest an event that could be used to promote the film. Decide which is your best event. Write a newspaper article to describe the event.

REMEMBER THIS

All the parts of the marketing mix are important to the success of a product. Promotion is the way that a business tells people that a product exists. It is also the way that the business tries to persuade people to buy its product. The main tools used in promotion are advertising and PR. The product needs to have the right price and the right promotion at each stage of the product life cycle.

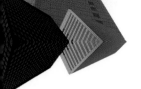
Unit 55 Branding and image

REVIEW THIS

Product, price and promotion are three important parts of the marketing mix. If a business can balance these correctly, then the product can be a success. Branding is part of the way in which a product is promoted. It is a way to give a product an image. Businesses hope that the image will then help to sell the product. Brands and brand image are so important to businesses that they are protected by law. A business that has spent a fortune building up an image for itself will fight any business that looks like it is 'stealing' the image.

READ THIS

Often a brand is so important to a business that it will go to court to protect it. mmO_2, the third largest mobile phone operator in the UK, did this with rival mobile group 3. 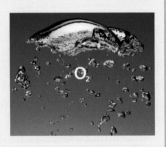 mmO_2 has created advertising and branding that uses images of bubbles, and has registered many images of bubbles as trade marks. These include special images of bubbles described as 'fizzing' and 'blasting'. It has used bubbles in its adverts since it broke away from BT in 2001. mmO_2 accuses 3 of using as many as 18 images of bubbles, which it claims it owns.

Almost everyone who is likely to buy a mobile phone in the UK now owns one already. This means that selling more phones is becoming more and more difficult. If you look back at Unit 52 you will see that this is a sign of a saturated market. When the market is 'full' like this, businesses have to go to great lengths to persuade people to buy. Brands and brand loyalty are therefore very important. mmO_2 takes its brand image very seriously and asked

the court to ban 3 from using the images. The company also asked that all the advertising material should be handed over. On the other hand, 3 says that it has not broken any rules. It claims that the bubble images it uses are its own.

THE BASICS

A **brand** is a trade name of a business. It is registered so that it can be used only by the business itself. It is not only brand names that are protected. The image of a business may be connected with a type of writing, such as the M in the McDonald's logo, or the way in which Coca-Cola is written. It could be a **slogan** like 'Heinz 57 Varieties' or 'Every little helps' (Tesco). It could even be the shape of a bottle (Coca-Cola again) that is protected. Even images used in adverts, like the bubbles used by mmO_2, could be part of a brand.

Brands are used so that people recognise products. They are used to create **brand loyalty**. This means that if a person finds good value in Heinz beans, they will also buy other Heinz products. Sometimes the brand is used to give the whole business an image, like Virgin. In other cases, each product has a brand name; for instance, washing powders like Daz, Persil and Ariel. Sometimes a brand is so strong that it is always linked to a certain product. Colman's mustard and Bird's custard are just two examples. Some brands have become so strong that they have become the normal word for a product. Biro is actually a brand name!

Often, the leading brands in a market are also the **market leaders**. In other words, they have the biggest share of the market. Brand loyalty is so important that many high-street chains and supermarkets now produce their own brands. Often they try to make these look like the leading brands. If they become too similar in appearance, there is usually a court case.

Continued →

LOOK AT THIS

Imagine you are selling a new mobile. This is what it looks like before it is branded. Remember, to sell at all in a saturated market, it must seem very special. You can make it special by giving it a good brand name and image.

1 Think up a brand name for the product. Use colour and design to give it a brand image. Copy the plan for the box on to a large sheet of paper. Add your brand design.

2 Describe which part of the market your mobile is aimed at.

3 Explain why you think your branding will appeal to that part of the market.

WORD BANK

Brand – a trade name or image of a business

Slogan – a phrase that is easy to remember and reminds you of a product

Brand loyalty – when a consumer buys because they like the image of the brand

Market leader – the business with the largest share of a market

REMEMBER THIS

Promotion is a vital part of the marketing mix. It is used to inform and persuade people. One part of promotion is the brand or image that a product has. Brands help people to spot products easily. They help businesses by creating brand loyalty. Brands are so important to businesses that it is normal to register them so that they are protected by law.

DO THIS

Some brands are so strong that consumers always think of them first. Look at the list of products given and decide which brand first comes to mind for each. Share your findings with a partner to see if you agree. Share the findings across your whole group. What does this tell you about the strength of brands?

- breakfast cereal
- burgers
- sportswear
- washing powder
- washing up liquid
- chocolate
- crisps
- coffee
- cola
- mobile phone

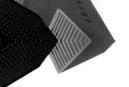

Unit 56 Distribution (place)

REVIEW THIS

For a product to be a success, the business must create the right mix of product, price and promotion. The product must be a quality one – that is, one that does its job well. The price must be one at which the buyer thinks they are receiving value for money. The promotion must inform the customer and persuade them to buy. All of these must be at the right level for each part of the product life cycle. There is one other important factor. The product must be easy to obtain. The final part of the marketing mix is 'place'.

READ THIS

The chain of supply proved to be of special importance to supermarket chain Sainsbury's in the winter of 2004. Problems with the supply of some of its goods meant that Sainsbury's posted a loss. It had never before made a loss in the 135 years since it was set up by John James and Mary Anne Sainsbury in 1869. The reason for the loss was clear. Customers were going to other stores because Sainsbury's was failing to stock certain essential items. In 1995, Sainsbury's had been the leading business in the retail food market. In September 2004, it dropped to third place behind Tesco and Asda. Tesco had 28 per cent of the market and Asda

Continued ➔

16.9 per cent of the market, with Sainsbury's on 15.3 per cent. Sainsbury's is even fighting to keep this place, as fourth-placed Morrisons also increased its share.

The problem at Sainsbury's appears to come from an attempt to computerise stock systems that has not worked. This meant that many stores were running out of items and shelves were left empty. To try and solve the problem, the store cut prices on over 6,000 items. It is also taking on 3,000 extra shop-floor staff to keep shelves stocked by hand. But this will only solve the problem in the short term. In the longer term, the store will need to find a permanent solution to its supply problems. It will also need to win back customer confidence that it really can supply them with what they need. (*Source: Independent*, 18 November 2004)

THE BASICS

Place is the final part of the marketing mix. It refers both to the places where a product is sold and to the way in which the product reaches them. The method by which a product reaches a place is called **distribution**. The **channel of distribution** is the name given to the way in which the product arrives from its maker (the producer) to you (the consumer). The full channel is:

Producer > Agent > Wholesaler > Retailer > Consumer

Any stage can be cut out to make the channel shorter. For instance, if you bought eggs from a farm, this is from producer direct to retailer.

Each business in the chain does a certain job. **Agents** sell products on behalf of producers. They get paid a share of the amount they sell. This is called commission. **Wholesalers** buy in large amounts and sell products on in smaller amounts. This is called **breaking bulk**. They also provide storage. **Retailers** sell direct to the consumer.

Products may be sold direct to the consumer from any part of the chain. Ways to do this include mail order and the internet.

'Place' is also used to describe the places where products are retailed. Sometimes this is a shop. These can be of many different types and sizes. Some sell only one sort of product. Others may sell many types of product. The important thing for businesses is to choose the right channel. For consumers, it is to know where they can buy products.

LOOK AT THIS

Many distribution channels are not just national, but international. The type of transport chosen will depend on the products being carried.

1 List products that would best be carried by each of plane, boat, ship, train and lorry.

2 Explain why your chosen method of transport is most suitable.

DO THIS

Businesses must take care to choose the right channel of distribution. Some products, like fresh food, need to be sold quickly. Others, like diamonds, need to be secure. Some, like shoes, can only really be sold direct to the consumer.

1 Draw up chains of distribution for five products. Each chain should cut out one or more of the stages.

2 Describe what is happening at each stage.

3 Explain why the chain you have drawn up would be suitable for the products chosen.

WORD BANK

Place – both the places where a product is sold and the way that the product reaches each place

Distribution – the method by which a product reaches a place

Channel of distribution – the stages the product passes through from producer to consumer

Agents – people or businesses that sell products on behalf of producers

Wholesalers – businesses that buy in large amounts and sell products on in smaller amounts

Breaking bulk – selling in small amounts products bought in large amounts

Retailers – businesses that sell direct to the consumer

REMEMBER THIS

For a business to be a success, it needs to have the right balance of product, price, promotion and place. These are the four parts of the marketing mix. At any stage in the life cycle of a product, a different mix may be needed. At any one time, any of the parts of the marketing mix may be the most important. Consumers will buy a product for many reasons. Some buy because the product is perfect for what they want. Some buy because the price is right. Some buy because they are persuaded by promotion. Some buy because it is easy or convenient for them to buy. A business has to balance all of these with its marketing mix to be a success

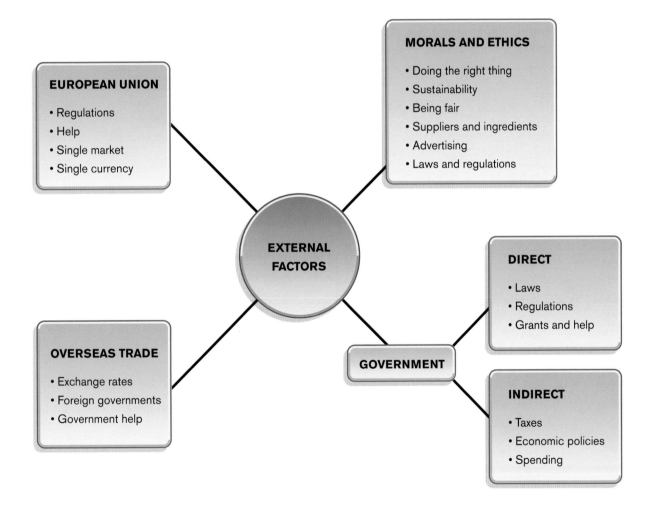

EUROPEAN UNION

- Regulations
- Help
- Single market
- Single currency

MORALS AND ETHICS

- Doing the right thing
- Sustainability
- Being fair
- Suppliers and ingredients
- Advertising
- Laws and regulations

EXTERNAL FACTORS

DIRECT

- Laws
- Regulations
- Grants and help

GOVERNMENT

INDIRECT

- Taxes
- Economic policies
- Spending

OVERSEAS TRADE

- Exchange rates
- Foreign governments
- Government help

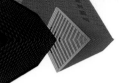

Unit 57 Business morals and ethics

REVIEW THIS

A business is often faced with choices. Should it make a certain product or not? Should it buy certain raw materials or not? Should it buy goods from certain countries or not? Its choices will be affected by **business ethics**. This means the moral point of view it takes. Some businesses may feel that it does not matter where products are made. A business may feel that it does not matter what workers' conditions are like or whether countries are getting a fair deal – as long as it is making a profit. Others have learned that more and more customers now expect businesses to act in a fair or moral way.

READ THIS

In January 2004, the *Guardian* newspaper carried out a survey for the magazine *Spark*. The survey asked over 1,000 people whether they thought that they acted ethically when buying goods and services. Over two-thirds said that they thought that they were green or ethical. They said that they looked for **organic food** or fair trade products (where the grower receives a fair part of the selling price). This was not just for food, either, but for many other things ranging from cars to insurance and pensions.

Young people, aged 18 to 34, were even more likely to be ethical spenders and use a wide range of shops. The UK has over 3,000 supermarkets selling fair trade products, and many more smaller, local shops. Sales of fair trade products reached over £100 million in 2004. The range of products has grown from just one brand of coffee a few years ago to over 130 foods. The range includes fruit and vegetables,

chocolate, juice, snacks, tea, sugar, honey, nuts and even wine. Harriet Lamb, director of the Fairtrade Foundation, said that the growth 'had developed out of new awareness that the world price of most foods is less than it was 20 years ago and that unfair trade has left hundreds of millions struggling to survive'. (*Source: Guardian*, 28 February 2004)

THE BASICS

Think about this. Tom and Tim are friends. Would it be right for Tom to steal Tim's pen? Would it be right for Tom to offer Tim less than it is worth to buy it? Would it be right for Tom to force Tim to sell it to him for less than it is worth?

Acting in an **ethical** way means trying to do the 'right' or 'moral' thing. It means, for instance, not taking advantage of someone just because they are weaker than you. In business terms, it means making decisions that are not going to cause harm. This includes both the people who supply the business and the people who buy from it. A business has to decide what products or services it will *buy*, what it will *make* and what it will *sell*.

When it buys products, an ethical business will make sure that it is:

- **paying a fair price to the people who have produced the goods**
- **not buying things whose production harms the environment**
- **not buying goods or services from businesses that do not give proper rights or working conditions to workers**

When it makes goods or services, it will make sure that:

- **it does not use processes that could cause harm to the environment**

Continued →

- it does not cause excess nuisance or pollution

- it gets rid of waste in a safe manner

- it gives its own workers proper rights and conditions

When it sells products it will make sure that:

- customers get a fair deal

- goods are safe to have and use

- it provides honest and clear labels and information.

It would also be unethical for a business to try unfair ways of competing with rivals, such as stealing their secrets or plans, or using their power to drive them out of markets.

DO THIS

Work with a partner. Draw up a four-column table with the headings 'product', 'problem', 'business response' and 'customer response'. Read the exchange in the cartoon. In your table, fill in the product and what you think is the problem or problems. (There may be more than one!) Now fill in what you would do in this situation if you were a business. Fold the paper so your partner cannot read what you have put. Swap papers and fill in what you would do as a customer. Open the paper out and read the two points of view. Is there a problem?

Agree with your partner what the business and the customer should do.

Think of other products and problems, and give a business and customer answer.

WORD BANK

Business ethics – making moral choices or decisions in the business world

Organic food – food grown without artificial fertiliser or additives

Ethical – taking the right or moral course of action is acting ethically

External influences – things that have an effect on the business but over which it has no control

REMEMBER THIS

There are a number of things that affect a business but over which it has little or no control. These are called external influences. The choices that consumers make are, more and more, taking account of how fairly, or ethically, products are made and sold. Many businesses have decided that 'doing the right thing' is good because consumers prefer to deal with ethical businesses.

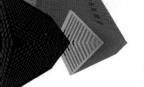
Unit 58 Business and government

REVIEW THIS

The main thing a business will try to do is make a profit. It can try to do this by being fair. In other words, it can behave ethically. Some businesses may not behave in a fair way. This is why there are laws and regulations. Businesses are directly affected by certain laws. They are also affected by other government policies. These will be trying to make a strong economy, create jobs and keep prices steady. All of these changes can have good or bad effects on business.

Sony plasma TV screen

READ THIS

Interest rate changes can hit some types of business much harder than others. Sometimes interest rates do not affect sales. This is usually the case in situations where a buyer has little choice whether or not to buy something. So, for instance, food sales will not be hit by higher rates. If buyers do have a choice of whether or not to buy, interest rate levels may carry a lot of weight. Some businesses sell mostly items that are of this type.

Sony is one of these businesses. It sells mainly high-priced electrical goods such as computers and televisions. These are called 'high ticket' goods, items where it is easy for a buyer to decide not to buy. In 2004, sales in the run-up to Christmas grew at the slowest pace all year. This

Continued ➜

was blamed on the five interest rate rises over the year. Items bought for the home, and electrical goods were the two areas that were worst hit. With many of these items, people would borrow money in order to buy them. As interest rates rise, they are less likely to do this.

When other companies lower price in order to compete, Sony must do the same. It might also gain from government policies such as the drive for digital television. At Christmas, there were record sales of digital boxes.

THE BASICS

Governments affect businesses in both direct and indirect ways. The main direct ways are through the use of laws to make sure that businesses act fairly. Where unfair competition might happen, there are controls. So, for instance, bodies such as the **Office of Fair Trading** (OFT) and **Competition Commission** are used to keep watch over business. Where a vital service – like water, gas or post – is in private hands, the government sets up **watchdogs**. These make sure that prices are fair and the service is good.

The government can also help businesses. It does this in direct ways. For instance, it has created special zones where businesses can set up more easily and cheaply. These are often in areas where there are few jobs. It can also give money such as **start-up grants**.

Governments also affect businesses in indirect ways through their policies. The government takes taxes to pay for services. It is also a major spender. Types and rates of tax affect whether people can afford to buy. They will also affect profit. Government spending (or lack of it) can affect how many jobs there are. A government policy can have an effect. Some, like the proposed switch to digital television, will be good news for some, bad news for others. Interest rates can also affect whether a person can afford to pay for something or not. Of course this has an effect on business. The Bank of England now sets the interest rate level each month. For instance, if it thinks the economy needs to slow down because people are spending too much, it will raise the rate.

LOOK AT THIS

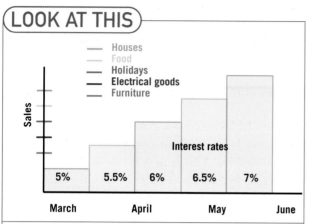

Look at the chart. It shows changes in interest rates.

1 Copy the graph out. Draw on it what you think happened to the sales of the items shown.

2 Outline why you think that sales moved this way.

3 Explain why the Bank of England might have raised interest rates in this way.

DO THIS

Write a simple explanation (that an 11-year-old could follow) for each of the following. You could write these on poster paper and use them for display. The first one has been completed to give you an idea of length and how easy the explanation should be.

○ borrow and lend

○ interest rates

○ discretionary purchase

○ government policies

Borrow and lend: *Sometimes people mix up 'borrow' and 'lend'. A bank has money. It lends it to me. As a customer I borrow from the bank. I am a borrower, it is a lender.*

WORD BANK

Office of Fair Trading – this provides help and advice to consumers; it produces leaflets and guides; it keeps a watch for consumer problems and may step in to solve them

Competition Commission – this government body keeps an eye on firms taking over other firms; it will act if it thinks that take-overs and other growth will be harmful to consumers

Watchdogs – these are also called regulators; they are independent bodies that make sure that prices are fair and that service is good

Start-up grants – special grants that are given to help new businesses get started

REMEMBER THIS

Businesses have to work within certain rules. Many of those rules are laid down by governments. They are meant to make sure that businesses do not act in an unfair way. Governments also have policies. These are to help the economy and certain groups within it. Businesses will be affected by changes in these policies. Sometimes they will gain from a change. At other times, they may lose.

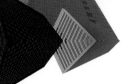

Unit 59 Business and the European Union

REVIEW THIS

There are various levels of government that affect business. There is the national level, the local level, and also international

bodies of which Britain is a member. These lay down rules that have to be followed. One of the bodies that has a big effect on Britain and on businesses in Britain is the European Union (EU). Rules are agreed by the members of the EU. All the members then have to abide by those rules if they want to gain the benefits of being a member.

READ THIS

In November 2004, the government revealed that the European Social Fund (ESF) would again be helping to create jobs in England. An extra £111 million was to be spent. The ESF is one of four funds set up by the European Union (EU). It promotes the teaching of knowledge and skills to help prepare people for the job market. It also aims to be of special help to women who want to work. The other three funds promote other areas. One is concerned with improving regions, such as through better roads and communications. One helps farmers and rural areas, and the other one helps those involved in fishing and fish breeding.

The Odyssey Trust in London is one of the projects sponsored by the ESF. It was set up to help drug users and people who have just come out of prison to secure jobs. It also provides advice and training to other groups who find it hard to cope with the job market. (*Source: Independent*, 25 November 2004)

THE BASICS

The **European Union** (EU) is made up of a number of countries that have decided to act together in many areas. These areas include a number of things that affect business. The main idea behind the EU was to free up trade. Trade between EU countries is now easier than it has ever been. In many countries, there are few, if any, border controls. This is as a result of the **single market** being set up in 1993.

Many of the countries in the EU have also adopted the euro (€), instead of their own currency. This is called the **single currency**. It was introduced in 1999. This has made trade between these countries even more easy. Britain is still deciding whether or not to adopt the euro.

The EU has been such a success that many other countries now want to join. The EU collects payments from its richer members. It uses these to give support to members where it thinks this is needed. Its aim is for all members to reach the same standards of living. The EU has also made laws that affect businesses. These include:

- letting workers travel to work in any member country
- protecting workers' rights
- setting the minimum wage that must be paid
- setting maximum working hours
- setting levels of pension
- encouraging businesses to let workers take part in decision-making.

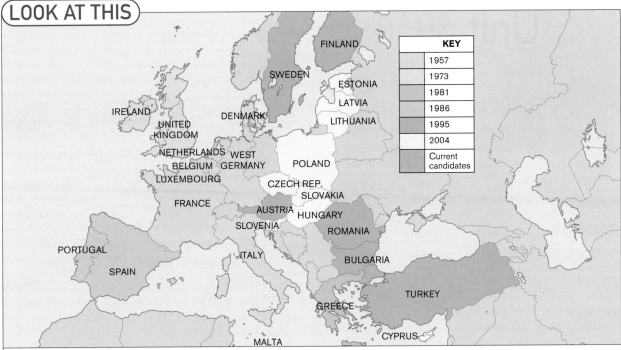

KEY	
	1957
	1973
	1981
	1986
	1995
	2004
	Current candidates

The picture shows how the EU has expanded from when it was first set up.

1 Draw a timeline to show how the EU has grown.

2 Look at the countries that have not joined. Explain why you think they prefer not to join.

3 Suggest reasons why those countries that are not yet members (in blue) want to join. Explain whether they should be allowed to join or not.

 DO THIS

The government is to ask people whether or not they want to get rid of the pound and replace it with the euro. Work in pairs.

1 List the reasons why people might want to keep the pound or join the euro.

2 Join with another pair to see if you have the same reasons. Decide whether you are for or against the change.

3 Produce a leaflet to try to persuade people to accept your point of view.

 **WORD BANK**

European Union – a 'club' of 25 member states, set up to make trade easier

Single market – created in 1993, this allows goods and labour to move freely around Europe

Single currency – the euro (€), set up in 1999; it is the currency used by many of the EU members, replacing their own currencies

 REMEMBER THIS

Governments affect business at many levels. These include local, national and international levels. The EU is an international body with 25 member countries. It was set up to promote trade between countries. It has brought Europe together to the extent that many countries now have few border controls. Also many countries use the euro. Some people agree with the EU and think it is a good thing; other people do not support it and would like Britain to leave.

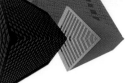

Unit 60 Overseas trade

REVIEW THIS

Businesses deal with many influences over which they have no control. These include government policies. They also include laws set by bodies like the EU. If trading overseas, they also include the laws and rules set by foreign governments. Trading using different currencies, languages and laws is harder than trading at home. Even though there are many different laws and rules, businesses still trade with other countries. This is because there is so much to be gained by overseas trade.

 READ THIS

Do you want to lose weight? Do you want to do it without having to cut down on the foods that you like? Then the giant food and soap firm Unilever may have the answer. It is already in the market for slimming aids through its Slim-Fast range. Now it has bought the rights to the rare hoodia cactus. This cactus grows in southern Africa. It has been used by the San bushmen of the region for hundreds of years. It is used to stop them from feeling hungry when food is scarce or when out hunting. Phytopharm is the name of the business that has been developing the cactus for use in foods. In trials it has been shown to reduce the number of calories that people eat.

The trade in the cactus should bring gains to all involved. The San bushmen will be paid for their plants. They will also be paid for their knowledge of how to use them. Countries such as the USA should gain from reduced health problems caused by obese people. Obesity is said to cost the USA more than £60 billion a year. This is through days lost at work due to illness and through the health costs of dealing with obese people. (*Source: Guardian*, 16 December 2004)

THE BASICS

Trade between countries brings many gains. Some countries have a better climate than others, so can grow certain things. Much of the fruit we now accept as common would not be in the shops if it were not for trade. Some countries have certain natural resources. These could include things that are found, like oil. Or they could be plants that grow, like the hoodia. Some countries train their workforce so that it is very good at certain things. A country will gain by trading what it can produce easily, for items that it either does not have or cannot produce easily or cheaply.

Exchange rates affect how well businesses can compete abroad. The state of the economy and levels of interest rates affect exchange rates.

If a business buys from abroad, this is an **import**. If a business sells to another country, this is an **export**. Goods can be seen, so are called **visible trade**. Services cannot be seen, so are called **invisible trade**. If the exchange rate is good, then it is harder to export, but easier to import. If you are not sure whether a good or service is an import or an export, look at the flow of money. For instance, if you buy a slimming product from Africa, you spend the money and they receive it. The money has gone from the UK to Africa, and the good has gone from Africa to the UK: an export for Africa, an import for the UK. If too much is spent abroad and less is spent at home this can cause problems. For instance, jobs may be created abroad but destroyed in the UK.

LOOK AT THIS

Draw a picture of a mobile phone in the centre of a sheet of poster paper. This could be one of the phones shown, or a better one.

1 Around it, show which country each part of the phone has come from. It will contain gold in the chips inside. It will be made of various metals, plastic and glass. It will use dyes (for printing labels and logos). Include as much as you can.

2 Which services do you think were involved in transporting the goods to the manufacturer?

3 Explain what this tells you about the importance of trade.

 DO THIS

Many businesses, even small ones, buy goods and services from abroad. Most consumers buy goods and services from abroad without even knowing.

Draw up two columns.

1 List the things you own that are around you. This will include your clothes, bag, pens, pencils, and so on.

2 In the next column, list which country you think each has come from. In many cases this will be more than one country. Labels on the goods may tell you where they are from.

3 The hoodia plant is just one example of a good that comes from abroad but brings us benefits. Look at your lists. Explain what you think you would have to do without if we did not trade overseas.

WORD BANK

Exchange rates – the rate at which £1 or €1 can be changed for another currency; if the pound or euro is strong, then it will buy more of a foreign currency; a strong pound means that goods from abroad (imports) are cheaper; goods being sold abroad (exports) will be more expensive

Import – when a good or service is bought from another country

Export – when a good or service is sold to another country

Visible trade – trade in goods, which can be seen

Invisible trade – trade in services, which cannot be seen

 ## REMEMBER THIS

Without overseas trade, we would not have many of the goods that we accept as common. Overseas trade allows us to exchange the goods and services that we can produce easily and cheaply with those that other countries can produce easily and cheaply. This means that each country benefits from the trade. There are many rules for businesses that trade overseas. This is to make sure that they are all trading fairly.

11 Succeeding

Unit 61 Preparing for the exam

There are a wide range of Business Studies courses at GCSE. One thing they all have in common is that they use an examination paper as part of their assessment. The style of the papers will vary and so will the type of question asked. Some papers may test a particular module or unit of work. Others may test the whole subject. Some examination boards set a problem-solving paper as an alternative to coursework. The amount of time varies from one hour up to two.

Most papers include questions or tasks that test your knowledge of business. These might be short questions asking you to recall your knowledge. Or they might include questions that ask you to use and apply your knowledge to business situations. Many questions expect you to select information from a piece of data and then use it in the answers. This is why you should always try to link your knowledge with the data to develop an explanation. Finally, some questions expect you to draw up some conclusions. To do this, you will have to compare solutions and weigh up their advantages and disadvantages. This will allow you to show that you have thought through the possible answers. This evaluation will help to gain important extra marks when you make your final conclusion.

KEY POINTS

Whatever type and style of examination paper you have to take, there are key points to remember and use.

- Do not use a pencil, red or green pen to write your answers. Most examiners actually prefer black ink to be used as it is easier to read. If you use blue ink, make sure it is a dark blue.

- Do not write in the margins and do not try to squash your answers in when you run out of lines. Use the extra blank pages at the back of the exam paper, or ask for additional sheets from the exam invigilators. If you use this stationery, make sure you number each response correctly.

- Do try to write clearly, as each year several candidates limit their possible marks because it is impossible to read some answers.

- Do read the question carefully and make sure you answer the question that is being asked – and not the one you would like it to be. This is particularly important when the question appears to be one that has been asked in the past.

- Do read the data carefully, as there may be clues to help your response. The question may require you to select specific information from the data.

- Use the number of marks per question to guide you on the length of response needed.

- Keep an eye on the time. If you do not answer all the questions, you will automatically reduce the marks you could possibly achieve.

- Always read the instructions on the front cover. They include important reminders before you start to put pen to paper.

- Each question will have a 'command' word that will be telling you how to frame your answer. This is particularly important for questions using 'explain', 'why', 'describe', 'analyse' or 'justify'. Answers to these questions mean that you have to make some points, but then you need to develop or expand them. You have to say something extra about the point without becoming repetitive. Using examples is one way to help you explain or develop an answer.

- Unless the question uses the command word 'list', always answer using sentences and paragraphs.

- Always try to use business terms rather than general words and phrases. For example, the word 'money' is often used by candidates when 'revenue', 'costs' or 'profit' would have been the correct business term.

- Try not to mix up terms such as 'borrow' and 'lend', 'price' and 'cost' or 'revenue' or 'profit'.

- Some candidates take three or four lines of writing before they actually start to answer the question. Do not rewrite the question, but try to find a quick way to introduce and start your answer. Remember, most introductions will not help you to score marks.

I must get up to speed writing these answers!

Candidates often ask what they should revise for Business Studies. The simple answer is always everything! It is impossible to 'spot' the question, but your teachers should be able to suggest the most important areas to cover in greatest depth.

'HOW SHOULD I REVISE?'

- While you will receive lots of general advice, it is important to ask your Business Studies teachers for specific advice.

- Make key notes of all your work so that you have definitions, examples, formulas for business calculations, lists of features and lists of advantages and disadvantages.

- Pin up your key notes around your bedroom so that you can picture the information when you are trying to remember it.

- Ask someone to test you on key knowledge – over and over again.

- Create your own ways to remember the most difficult parts – little sayings or even songs or chants which you can say to yourself!

- Finally, keep practising exam questions and have them marked so that you know how to improve.

Unit 62 Exam paper features

Whichever Business Studies course you are following, you will need to be familiar with the style of the examination paper. Ask your teachers to show you past papers. If the course is new, the exam board will have created a specimen paper which will show you the planned style. You need to look at the paper carefully and notice, in particular, the instructions, the data and the style of questions. This unit tries to explain some of the likely features of examination papers.

Most papers have a front cover with space for you to put your name, centre, centre number and candidate number. Many exam boards now expect you to write in your signature to say that it is your work. The front cover usually has a list of 'instructions to candidates' which you need to read before the examination starts. Make sure you read and carry out the instructions.

DEALING WITH DATA

Most examination papers then give you some data that introduces the real world context for the questions. You are likely to be given background information about the type of business or organisations, the products sold and quite probably some of the people working for the business. Read this carefully as you may be able to use some of it in answers to questions. In some papers, all of the data is given to you before any questions are asked. In other papers, some data will be given followed by some questions, and then further data and questions will follow.

Data may be presented in different ways:

○ **You may have some pictures or illustrations.**

○ **You will be given pieces of text to read.**

○ **Sometimes this text may be presented in speech bubbles, or as an extract from a newspaper.**

○ **Part of the data will almost certainly include financial figures and even some accounts.**

However it is presented, always take time to read and look at the data carefully.

A question that is testing your knowledge might be worded:

'Using examples, explain the term 'fixed costs'. (4 marks)'

To gain full marks, you need to give a definition and support this with two examples. If you can, link the examples to the business in the exam case study. A sample answer might be:

'Fixed costs do not change when output varies. They have to be paid even when nothing is made. Rent and insurance for a building are examples, as they will have to be paid even if the business has no customers.'

CALCULATIONS

Calculation questions are asked in most papers. A typical example might read:

'Showing your working, calculate Colin's gross profit for 2004. (4 marks)'

It is important that you use a calculator so that your answer is exact. You must always set out your workings to show how you have arrived at the answer. Normally, as long as you have clearly shown the correct answer, you will gain full marks. If you do not have the correct answer, the examiner may still be able to give you some marks for knowing part of the process.

Some questions will test your ability to evaluate and draw conclusions. A possible example might be worded:

'Carol wants to increase the theatre's profit. She has three options:

- ○ **serve hot meals**
- ○ **hold weekly bingo**
- ○ **sell season tickets.**

Compare the three options and advise Carol on the best way for her to increase the theatre's profit. (12 marks)'

You need to discuss the advantages and disadvantages of each option. You need to show how revenue might be helped, how costs might be affected and therefore how profits might be improved. You must make sure that you suggest which option would be best, and you must give reasons to support this. There is rarely a correct answer. The examiners just want to mark you on your ability to use your business knowledge to solve a problem.

COMPLETING DOCUMENTS

On some papers you might be asked to complete business documents or accounts using data and information given in a question. Take great care that you put the right data item in the right place. When putting numbers in place, make sure you copy figures accurately.

Take great care with the number of 'noughts' in a figure. Once you have completed the document or account, always check to see that what you have done makes sense.

CASE STUDIES

Examination papers are sometimes an alternative to coursework. These test you in the same way, but instead of having to collect data, you will be given a whole case study. You have to read this and then interpret the data in the case study. The task will ask you to solve some sort of problem for the business, and may be quite structured. You will need to select and use parts of the data together with your business knowledge. Try to link parts of the data together to build up a picture of the business in the case study. Always keep your conclusions realistic and sensible.

PRACTICE MAKES PERFECT

As well as looking at examination papers, it is vital that you have plenty of exam practice. You need to become used to answering questions under exam conditions. It is important that you know how long to take answering each question so that you work under a time restraint. When you receive your marked work back, pay most attention to how you can improve your marks. Ask your teachers how the questions are marked. Share your answers with other people in your class. You can all learn good ideas from each other.

Unit 63 Coursework: Single Award GCSE

The form that your Single Award GCSE coursework will take depends very much on your chosen examination board. Most of your GCSE will be tested through an examination, but up to 25 per cent of the marks may be gained through coursework. The two main types are:

1 **Portfolio work. This is a collection of pieces of work to show a deeper knowledge and understanding of a particular part of a specification.**

2 **Single piece work. This a single, extended piece of coursework. It could be as much as 3,000 words long. It can be used to show deeper understanding of a wide part of the specification.**

CHOICE

For most examination boards, there is an examination paper alternative to coursework. This means that, if you do not think you will do very well at coursework, you can take a test instead. You can make this decision quite late in the course, when

you see how well your coursework has turned out. The main boards options are shown below.

WHY DO COURSEWORK?

Before you make your decision, you should think about the possible benefits of doing coursework.

○ **It will normally allow you to specialise in an area in which you are interested.**

○ **Your teacher can look at it and give you advice. You can then go away and improve it as many times as you wish.**

○ **You can receive help and information from all sorts of people and sources, e.g. libraries, councils, newspapers, relatives, friends, teachers and the internet.**

○ **It is possible to receive full marks on coursework. This means that, combining it with the examinations, it may be easier for you to reach a top grade.**

Board	Coursework	Option to take test
AQA (Specification A)	Either a single piece or portfolio work, based on certain subject areas set by the board	No
AQA (Specification B)	A single piece, based on any part of the content	Yes – 1 hour
AQA Short	A single piece, based on any part of the content	Yes – 1 hour
Edexcel Full	A report, based on a chosen area of content	No
Edexcel Short	A report, based on a chosen area of content	No
OCR (Specification A)	An investigation into an area chosen by the board	Yes – 1 hour 30 minutes
OCR (Specification B)	An investigation into an area chosen by the board	No
OCR Short	An investigation into an area chosen by the board	Yes – 1 hour 30 minutes

- You may find it easier to work at your own pace and in the places that you want to work.

- It gives you the opportunity to go out and collect real information, e.g. on visits or surveys, or carrying out observations or interviews.

- It helps you to make the connections between the different parts of the course and to see the 'whole picture' of business.

MARKS

Whichever type of coursework you do, for whichever board, it is generally marked in the same way. You will need to show that you can:

- Design your own research, so that you can collect information and evidence on your chosen topic.

- Organise the evidence that you have collected.

- Select the most useful evidence and use it. You should also be able to say why you have selected certain types of evidence and not others.

- Present the evidence that you have collected in different ways. You can use, for instance, charts and graphs, photographs and pictures, diagrams and maps as well as writing.

- Turn the raw data that you have collected into evidence. This means writing it up in a way that anyone should be able to understand.

- Use the specialist terms and language that are used in the world of business. For example, if you are talking about what a business owes, this is 'liability'; if you are talking about how a business aims products at different types of customer, this is 'market segmentation'.

- Use the concepts, ideas and methods that you have learned in the course. Can you show how a business might break even by using a chart, for example?

- Come to conclusions that are based on the evidence that you have collected. For example: 'I think that' ... 'because' ... 'and here is the evidence I base my view on ...'

FORMAT

Your coursework could take the following format. Check first to make sure that it fits in with what your board needs from you.

PURPOSE OF INVESTIGATION

In general, your coursework will be an investigation of a business problem or issue. You should start by saying what it is that you are investigating, and why. You can also say what you expect to find out. (It does not matter if you are later proved wrong by the information you collect).

PRIMARY RESEARCH

You will need to decide what information you want, and then by which methods you are going to collect it. Do not forget that there are many different ways to carry out primary research (see Unit 47), and you can use whichever is appropriate. Questionnaires, surveys, photographs, diagrams, interviews, taste tests, traffic and footfall counts and so on are all forms of primary investigation. It is important to plan what you need to find out first; it is also important to test tools (like surveys) before carrying them out.

SECONDARY RESEARCH

Secondary research also needs to be planned. It will be much easier if you have a good idea of what you are looking for before you start. For example, a tightly focused search on the internet can be very quick and give really good results. On the other hand, a general search can produce mountains of useless information.

ANALYSING RESEARCH

You will need to look at all the research evidence that you have collected and decide which of it is likely to be useful and why. If you can explain why you have not used certain items, this will boost your mark. Perhaps, information was old or out of date; perhaps it did not exactly fit what you needed. Look at the problems of research in Unit 47 to help you.

CONCLUSIONS AND JUDGEMENTS

Remember, there is not necessarily a right or wrong answer to the problem or issue you are looking at. To gain top marks, what you have to do is to justify why you have come to a particular conclusion. Your opinions, ideas and solutions are just as good as anyone else's. as long as you have backed them up with good evidence.

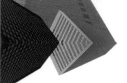

Unit 64 Coursework: Double Award Applied GCSE

The main part of the assessment for the Applied GCSE is through your coursework. You will need to put together two portfolios of work, one for Unit 1 and one for Unit 2. A portfolio is a collection of work which shows that you understand what you have been taught. Even more importantly, for the Applied GCSE, you must show that you can link what you have been taught, to businesses in the real world.

You will study a number of businesses to help you to do this. These may be businesses that you find for yourself, or businesses provided by your teachers. In either case, they should be businesses, from which you can get real information. It is no use, for example, trying to do the whole course based on the website of a business.

For Unit 1, you will study two businesses. This will help you to understand how the different parts of a business work together, and what may be possible to make it more efficient, or to help it make more profit. This will help you to see that there are different types and sizes of business, and that they have different aims. It will help you to see both the similarities and the differences between businesses.

For Unit 2, you study one business in detail. This gives you a better idea of how a business works. It is particularly concerned with the people side of business, looking at:

○ **the various groups of people who are affected by the operation of the business**

○ **how people are recruited**

○ **how the business protects their health and safety**

○ **their responsibilities and rights**

○ **the customers that are needed by business**

○ **how they are protected.**

DOING WELL

○ To enter the basic level, you need to **describe** what is happening.

○ To enter the middle level you need to **explain** what is happening. Key words will be 'because', 'as', 'so' and 'therefore'.

○ To hit the top level you need to **analyse** what is happening. You could say 'on the one hand, this information is good, or useful, because ...' but 'on the other hand, it is not as good because ...'.

You will be marked on how well you hit the targets set by the examination boards. These are slightly different for each board, so you will need to check which board you are following to make sure you do your best. They are all based, however, on the same areas.

KNOWLEDGE AND UNDERSTANDING

You must show the board that you know the subject matter and understand what you are talking about. You will be taught some of the knowledge by your teachers. You may pick up other key knowledge from the businesses that you are studying.

USING TERMS AND CONCEPTS

You must not only understand the terms, concepts and ideas that you have learned, but be able to apply them to the businesses that you are studying. You must use the proper business terms wherever possible. So you would refer to a person running a business on their own as a 'sole trader', or to the items owned by a business as 'assets'. You should use the methods that you have been taught to suggest ways of tackling problems or dealing with issues at the businesses you are studying.

PLANNING AND CARRYING OUT INVESTIGATIONS

You must plan your own investigations of issues at your chosen businesses. You must then carry out the investigations. You will need to collect information and show which of it you found useful. You should be able to say why the information you selected was of use, and why you rejected other information.

WEIGHING UP EVIDENCE, MAKING JUDGEMENTS AND PRESENTING CONCLUSIONS

For the top marks, you need to be able to analyse the evidence which you collect. One way to do this is by having a balance of opinion. You can then come to a conclusion.

UNIT 1

For Unit 1, you need to choose two different businesses. These may be different sizes, operating in different markets, or have different types of ownership. You will find the portfolio work easier if they have as many differences as possible. It is important that you can gain access to the businesses to talk to people. Smaller businesses, for example, may not have such things as printed aims or organisation charts. This means that you will need to find these out for yourself. Having a relative or friend who works at a business may help. You could also use your work experience business as one of the businesses to study.

Your Unit 1 portfolio could be broken down to describe, for each business:

- its main activities, aims and objectives
- the type of ownership and why it suits the business

- the liabilities of the owners
- the organisational structure
- what the functional areas do, and how they do it
- how the main functional areas work and communicate together
- how the business communicates both internally and externally
- where it is located and why
- the main competitors, and how they compete
- the other constraints on operation, such as legal and environmental factors.

UNIT 2

For Unit 2, you need to produce a portfolio based on your investigation of a medium- to large-sized business. You must choose a business that has at least three levels – e.g. manager, supervisor and worker. It must also have at least three people at one of the levels. This is so that you can investigate different job roles. Before choosing your business, you should have a really good look at what you have to do to make sure that it can provide you with all the information you need. Being half-way through the work and then finding that your chosen business is not suitable is a waste of time.

Your Unit 2 portfolio could be broken down to describe, for your chosen business:

- its main stakeholders and their aims
- how these aims might conflict and how such conflicts might be solved
- how it is organised and whether this suits it
- the roles, rights and responsibilities of workers in one of the main functional areas
- a comparison of the working roles, arrangements and rewards for different workers
- how it could benefit from flexible working arrangements.
- the main laws and health and safety issues that apply to it;
- the groups or unions that exist and how they can help workers
- how it deals with problems, grievances and disputes.

Index

Note: page numbers in **bold** refer to Word Bank terms.

ACAS (Advisory, Conciliation and Arbitration Service) 86, **87**
accountants 52
  chief 52
  cost 52
  management 52
accounting
  financial 53, **53**
  management 53, **53**
accounts *see* finance and accounts
acid test ratio 71, **71**
administration 14–15, 72
advertising 124, 125
  costs of 72, 73
  customer protection from 114, 115
  definition **125**
  jobs in 104
Advertising Standards Authority (ASA) 114
Advisory, Conciliation and Arbitration Service
  see ACAS
after-sales service 111, **111**
agents 128, **129**
aims, business 4, 6–7, 48, 49
Airbus 58, 59
analysts 104
application forms 82, **82**
artists 104
ASA *see* Advertising Standards Authority
Asda 18, 128
assets 39, **39**, 66
  current 66, 67, **67**, 70–1
  fixed 66, **67**
  net current 66, **67**
  net employed 66, **67**
assisted areas 97, **97**
auditors 53, **53**
authority 13, **13**

balance sheets 66–7, 70
Bank of England 135
banks 8, 98
  loans 4, **5**, 55, 69–70
bar code scanners 33
batch production 94, 95, **95**
BBC *see* British Broadcasting Corporation
benefits
  redundancy 2, **3**, 86, **87**
  work-related 25, **25**, 78–9
Board of Directors 13, 14
bonus payments 25, 72, 79
borrowed funds 55, **55**
  see also loans
BP (British Petroleum) 44
brand loyalty 126, **127**
branding 118, 119, 126–7, **127**
  global brands 44, **45**
Branson, Richard 36
break-even point 58–9, **59**
  contribution formula 59, **59**
  graphs 58–9
breaking bulk 128, **129**
British Broadcasting Corporation (BBC) 42, 49
brownfield sites 96, **97**
budgets 64–5
Bulb Media 48
bulk buying 17
Burger King 42
business

external influences on 131–9, **133**
  failure 2–3
  market oriented 105, **105**
  product orientated 104, **105**
business aims 4, 6–7, 48, 49
business ethics 132–3, **133**, 134
business growth 7, 18–19
  external 18
  internal 18, **18**
business objectives 4, 6–7
  SMART objectives 7
business organisation *see* organisation
business plans 2, 4–5
business size 16–17
business start-ups 2–3
business types 35–49
  charities 48–9
  cooperatives 48–9, **49**
  franchises 42–3, **43**
  holding companies 44–5, **45**
  limited liability companies 40–2, 44–5, 66, 69
  multinationals 44, 45, **45**
  partnerships 38–40, 42, 44–5, 54, 68
  public sector 46–7
  sole traders 36–7, **37**, 40, 42, 44–5, 54, 68, 104
  voluntary groups 48–9
buyers 104
buying (purchasing) 93
  bulk 16–17
  on credit 115
  ethical 132

Caffè Nero 72
calculations 144–5
call centres 76
candidates 80, **81**
Canon 32
canteens 79
capital 53, **53**, 66, 67, **67**
cars, company 79
case studies 145
cash flow forecasts 64–5
cash inflow 64, 65, **65**
cash outflow 64, 65, **65**
cash shortage 64, **65**
cash surplus 64, **65**
cashiers, chief 53
catalogues 31
caveat emptor 114, **115**
CBI *see* Confederation of British Industry
chain of command 13, 93
chain of production 90–1
chain of supply 128
change
  expected 26
  external 26
  internal 26
  unexpected 26
change management 26–7
  controlling change 27, **27**
  implementation of change 27, **27**
  planning for change 27, **27**
  reviewing change 27, **27**
channels of distribution 128–9, **129**
charities 48–9
Charity Commissioners 48
cheques 61, **62**, 63
chocolate industry 90, 106, 108
Christmas 124

Citroën 73
civil service 46, **47**
cleaning 15
clerical tasks 14
coalmining 97
Coffee Republic 72
coffee shops 72
collective bargaining 86, **87**
command, chain of 13, 93
commission 25
communication 22
  external 30–1
  information technology's support of 32–3
  internal 28–9
  inward 30, **31**
  outward 30, **31**
communication channels 28, **29**
  formal 28, **29**, 30–1
  informal 28, **29**, 30
  oral 28–9, 30–1
  written 29, 31
communications 56
communities 9
companies **41**
  holding 44–5, **45**
  limited liability 40–2, 44–5, 66, 69
  profit and loss accounts 68
Companies House 41
company secretaries 14, 15, **15**
competition 9
  market planning for 106, 107
  through pricing 72, 122, 123
  unfair 134
Competition Commission 134, **135**
Confederation of British Industry (CBI) 78, **79**, 86, **87**
confidentiality 33
conglomerate integration 19, **19**
Connex 42, 43
consumer co-ops 48, **49**
consumer protection 114–15
consumer protection acts 114, **115**
consumers 114, **115**
continuous flow (mass production) 95, **95**
contracts of employment 84, **85**, 86
contribution formula 59, **59**
control, span of 13, **13**
cooperatives 44, 48–9
  consumer co-ops 48, **49**
  mutuals 48, **49**
  producer co-ops 48, **49**
  worker co-ops 48, **49**
coordination 23, **23**
cost accountants 52
cost plus pricing 122, **123**
cost of sales 68, 69, **69**
Costa 72
costs 56–7
  and break-even 58, 59
  fixed 56, 57, **57**, 58, 59
  and industry location 96
  overheads 56, **57**, 72, 122, **123**
  and pricing 122, 123
  and quality 100
  reducing 72, 73
  running 56, **57**
  start-up 56, **57**
  total 57, **57**, 98
  unit 57, **57**, 72, 98–9, 122, **123**
  variable 56, 57, **57**, 58, 59
cotton industry 97

council tax 46
councils 14
coursework 146–9
  analysing research 147
  benefits of 146–7
  choice regarding 146
  conclusions and judgements 147, 149
  doing well 148
  Double Award GCSE 148–9
  format 147
  knowledge and understanding 148
  marking 147
  planning and carrying out investigations 149
  portfolio work 146, 148
  primary research 147
  purpose of investigation 147
  secondary research 147
  Single Award GCSE 146–7
  single piece work 146
  terms and concepts 149
  Unit 1 149
  Unit 2 149
credit, buying on 115
credit cards 106
credit controllers 52
credit facilities 111, **111**
credit notes 61, **62**, 63
creditors 9, 66, **67**
current ratio 70–1, **71**
curriculum vitae see CV
customer loyalty 110, 111, **111**, 113
customer profiles 106–7, **107**
customer satisfaction 112–13, **113**
customer service 33, 110–11
  after-sales service 111, **111**
  giving advice 110
  information provision 110, 111
  providing ways to pay 111
customers 8
  definition 114
  and ethical business 133
  happy 110, 111, 112–13
CV (curriculum vitae) 80, 81, 82, **83**

data
  dealing with in exams 142, 144
  handling 32–3
  marketing 104, **105**, 108, 109, **109**
  processing 14
  storage 32–3
databases 32–3
debtors 66, **67**
debts, measuring ability to pay 70–1
decision making 22–3, 26–7, 136
  operational 26, **27**
  in partnerships 38, 39
  of sole traders 36, 37
  strategic 26, **27**
  tactical 26, **27**
Deed of Partnership 38–9, **39**, 40
delayering 13, **13**
delegation 13, **13**
delivery notes 60, 61, **62**, 63
designers 104
desktop publishing 32
direct mail 124, **125**
disabilities 85
disciplinary procedures 76, 84, **85**
discrimination 84–5, **85**
distribution see place (distribution)
Dixons 120
documents 29, 31, 60–3
Dyson, James 2

email 32
employees 8
  definition **85**
  and industrial relations 86, 87
  and performance measures 70

rights and responsibilities 84–5, 132, 133, 136
employers
  definition **85**
  and industrial relations 86, 87
  rights and responsibilities 84–5
employment, contracts of 84, **85**, 86
enterprise 1–9
  business aims and objectives 6–7
  business planning 4–5
  stakeholders 8–9
  starting a business 2–3
entrepreneurs 2, 3, **3**, 8, 91
environmental issues 132–3
equal rights 84–5
equipment 56, 68, 69, 92
ethical action 132–3, **133**
euro 136
European Social Fund 136
European Union (EU) 136–7, **137**, 138
exams 142–6
  calculations 144–5
  case studies 145
  completing documents 145
  dealing with data 142, 144
  exam paper features 144–5
  practice 145
  preparation 142–3
  revision tips 143
exchange rates 138, **139**
expenses 68–9, **69**
exports 138, **139**
external influences on business 131–9, **133**
  business morals and ethics 132–3
  the European Union 136–7
  governments 134–5
  overseas trade 138–9

fair trade 132
film industry 124–5
finance and accounts 31, 51–73
  balance sheets 66–7
  break-even point 58–9, **59**
  budgets 64–5
  cash flow forecasts 64–5
  costs 56–7
  the finance function 52–3
  financial documents 60–3
  improving profitability 72–3
  profit and loss accounts 68–9
  raising finance 54–5
  ratios 70–1
  revenue 56–7
  staff 52–3
financial accounting 53, **53**
financial documents 60–3
  cheques 61, **62**, 63
  credit notes 61, **62**, 63
  delivery notes 60, 61, **62**, 63
  goods received notes 61, **62**, 63
  purchase orders 60, **62**, 63
  receipts 62, **62**, 63
  remittance advice slips 61–2, **62**, 63
  sales invoices 60–1, **62**, 63
  statements of account 62, **62**, 63
financial planning 4
flexible working 78, **79**
food scares 94
Ford 18, 44
franchisees 42–3, **43**
franchisers 42–3, **43**
franchises 42–3, **43**, 44
fringe benefits (perks) 25, **25**, 78–9
fuel 72
furniture manufacturing 90

Gap 44
gap in the market 104, **105**
gender discrimination 85
global brands 44, **45**

go-slows (working slowly) 86
goods 36, **37**, 138
goods received notes 61, **62**, 63
governments 134–5
  policies 134–5
  regulations 134, 135
grants 54–5, **55**
  start-up 134, **135**
graphs, break-even 58–9
greenfield sites 96, **97**
growth, business 7, 18–19, **18**

hardware 32, **33**
Hardy, Rick 64
health care schemes 79
health and safety 84, 85
Health and Safety at Work Act 84, **85**
hierarchical organisations 13
Hit Entertainment 40
holding companies 44–5, **45**
holidays 76
Hoover 2
horizontal integration 18, **19**
Hornby 118, 119
housebuilding 92
HSBC 76
human resources 75–87
  the human resources function 76–7, **77**
  industrial relations 86–7
  job applications 82–3
  pay and benefits 78–9
  recruitment 80–1
  retention 80–1
  rights and responsibilities at work 84–5
  training 80–1

image 126–7
imports 138, **139**
income 4, **5**, 7, 16
Incredibles, The (film, 2004) 124–5
independence 7
India 76
inductions 81, **81**
industrial disputes 76, 86, 87, **87**
industrial relations 86–7, **87**
information and communications technology
  (ICT) 15, 32–3
Inland Revenue 69
innovation 99, **99**
insurance 68, 72
integrated information systems 32, **33**
interest 56, 72
interest rates 134–5, 138
internet 32, 33, 129
interviews 80, 82
intranets 32, 33
investment 69
invisible trade 138, **139**
invoices 31
iron 97

Jaguar 18
JD Wetherspoon 122
job applications 82–3
  applicants 80, **81**
  application forms 82, **82**
  application letters 80, 81, 82, **83**
job interviews 80, 82
job production 94, **94**, 95
job vacancies 80, **81**
JobCentres 82
just-in-time production 95, **95**

Kaizen 101, **101**
Kell and McGrane Ltd 60–2
Kellogg's 44, 104, 105
Kodak 86

labour turnover 76, **77**
land, costs 56

large businesses 16–17
laws 134, 135
leadership 22–3, **23**
  autocratic leaders 23
  democratic leaders 23
  laissez-faire leaders 23
leaflets 31
legal services 15
letters 29
  of application 80, 81, 82, **83**
  of enquiry 31
liabilities
  current 66, 67, **67**, 70–1
  long-term 66, 67
liability
  limited 40–1, **41**
  unlimited 36, **37**, 38, **39**, 40
limited liability companies 40–1, 44, 45
  private 40–1, 66
  public 40, 41, 42, 69
Livingstone, Ken 46
loans 4, **5**, 55, 56, 69–70
location of industry 96–7
  closeness to raw materials/markets 96
  cost of the site 96
  geographical influences on 96
  and the workforce 96
  see also land, costs; place (distribution)

machinery 92, 95
  and productivity 98, 99
  and quality of production 100, 101
mail handling 14
mail order 129
maintenance 15, **15**, 72, 92
management 21–33
  and accounts 52, 67
  chain of 22, **23**
  of change 26–7
  coordination role 23, **23**
  cycle of 22–3, **23**
  and decision making 22–3, 26–7
  and internal communication 28–9
  levels of 22
  motivating role 24–5
  and performance measures 70
  of production 93
  as shareholders 8
  styles of 22–3
management accounting 52, 53, **53**
manufacturing methods 94–5
mark-up 122, **123**
market leaders 126, **127**
market oriented businesses 105, **105**
market research 104, 108–9
  desk (secondary) research 108–9, **109**, 110
  field (primary) research 109, **109**, 110
market saturation 120, 121, **121**
market share 16, 112
  definition **7**, **17**, **113**
  maintaining 6
market trends 105, **105**
marketing agencies 104, **105**
marketing mix 114, 117–29
  branding 126–7, **127**
  place 122–3, 128–9, **129**
  pricing 122–4, 126, 128–9
  product 118–19, **119**, 120–4, 126, 128–9
  product life cycles 120–1
  promotion 122–9, **125**
marketing and sales 103–15
  consumer protection 114–15
  customer profiles 106–7
  customer satisfaction 112–13
  customer service 110–11
  market planning 106–7
  market research 108–9
  marketing and sales function 104–5
  see also sales

materials 92
  and product quality 101
  purchasing 93
  raw 56, 90, 91, 96
maternity leave 77, **77**
McDonald's 42, 44
media 124, **125**
  broadcast 124
  printed 124
medium-sized businesses 16
meetings 30
memoranda (memos) 29
mergers 18, **19**
MFI 52
mind maps (spider diagrams) 29
minimum wage 86, 136
`minutes' 29
mission statements 6
mobiles 112
Monstermob 112
morals, business 132–3, **133**, 134
Morrisons 128
motivation 24–5
multinationals 44, 45, **45**
mutuals 48, **49**

National Health Service (NHS) 78
NatWest 18
Nestlé 44
Nestlé Rowntree 108
Network Rail 42
networking 30, **31**
News Corporation Ltd 45
Nike 44
Nissan 44, 54, 96
non-profit-making organisations 42, 48–9

obesity 138
objectives
  business 4, 6–7
  SMART 7
Odyssey Trust 136
Office of Fair Trading (OFT) 134, **135**
offshoreing 76
Ofgas 47
Ofwat 47
operational decision making 26, **27**
operations function (production department)
  92–3
oral communication 28–9, 30–1
order forms 31
organic food 132, **133**
organisation, business 11–19
organisational charts 12–13
organisational pyramids 13
organisational structure 12, **13**
output 57, **57**, 92
overdrafts 55, 65
overheads 56, **57**, 72, 122, **123**
overseas trade 136–7, 138–9
overtime 24–5, 78, **79**
  refusal to work 86
owners' funds 54, **55**
ownership 8, 42
  of franchises 42, 43
  of limited liability companies 40
  of partnerships 38
  and performance measures 70
  sole traders and 36

packaging 92, 118, 119
partnerships 38–9, 42, 44, 45
  Deed of Partnership 38–9, **39**, 40
  liability status 38, **39**, 40
  profit and loss accounts 68
  raising finances 54
paternity leave 77, **77**
pay 76, 78–9
  bonus payments 25, 72, 79

overtime 24–5, 78, **79**
  rates of 78
  schemes 24–5
pay in instalments 111, **111**
pensions 76, 79, 136
performance measures
  profit and loss accounts as 69
  ratios as 70–1
perks see fringe benefits
Pfizer group 100
pharmaceutical industry 95, 100
photography 86
piece work 24, 78, **79**
Pixar 124
Pizza Hut 42
place (distribution) 122, 123, 128–9, **129**
  channels of distribution 128–9, **129**
  see also land, costs; location of industry
point-of-sale material 110, **111**
pollution 133
`post-its' 29
pottery industry 97, 100
power 56, 68, 69, 72
price per unit 59
price wars 72, 122
pricing 72, 118, 122–4, 126, 128–9
  business plans and 4
  cost plus 122, **123**
  fair 132
  mark-up 122, **123**
private limited companies 40–1, 66
private sector 44, **45**, 46
privatised industries 46, 47, **47**
producer co-ops 48, **49**
producers 128
product 118–19, **119**, 122–4, 126, 128–9
  core 73, **73**
  market research into 108
  new 73
  quality 119, **119**
  range 118, **119**
product development 118–19
product differentiation 118, **119**
product diversification 19, 73, **73**
product extension strategies 120, **121**
product life cycles 120–1, **121**
  explosive 120, **121**
  extended 120, **121**
  stages 120, 121
product maps 106, **107**
product orientated businesses 104, **105**
production 89–101
  batch production 94, 95, **95**
  chain of command 93
  chain of 90–1
  continuous flow 95, **95**
  controlling 92
  efficiency 98–9
  ethical 132–3
  job production 94, 95, **95**
  just-in-time 95, **95**
  location of industry 96–7
  manufacturing methods 94–5
  operations function (production department)
    92–3
  primary 91, **91**
  quality 100–1
  secondary 91, **91**
  tertiary 91, **91**
production lines 93, **93**
production operatives 93, **93**
production supervisors 93, **93**
productivity 98, **99**
productivity deals 98, **99**
profit 2, 4, 134
  definition **3**, **17**
  gross 68, 69, **69**
  gross profit ratio/margin 70, 71, **71**
  maximisation 6, 72–3

measurement 70
  as measurement of business size 16, **17**
  net 68–9, **69**
  net profit ratio/margin 70, 71, **71**
  partnerships and 39
  and pricing 122, 123
  public-sector 46–7
  retained 54, **55**
  sole traders and 36, 37
  see also non-profit-making organisations
profit and loss accounts 68–9
profit sharing schemes 79, **79**
promotion 72–3, 104, 122–9, **125**
  advertising 72, 73, 114, 115, 124, **125**
  business plans for 4
  public relations 124–5, **125**
protective clothing 79
public houses (pubs) 122
public limited companies 40, 41, 42, 69
public relations 124–5, **125**
public sector 46–7, **47**
purchase orders 60, **62**, 63
purchasing *see* buying

quality 92, 100–1, 119, **119**
  assurance 100, **101**
  and consumer protection 114, 115
  control 100, **101**
  Kaizen 101, **101**
  levels required by customers 100
  levels required by law 100
  statistical process control 100, **101**
  total quality management 101, **101**

racial discrimination 85
rates 68, 69, 72
ratios 70–1
  acid test ratio 71, **71**
  current ratio 70–1, **71**
  gross profit ratio/margin 70, 71, **71**
  net profit ratio/margin 70, 71, **71**
raw materials 56, 90, 91, 96
receipts 62, **62**, 63
reception 14
recruitment 80–1, **81**
redundancy 54, 76, 77, 86
  benefits 2, **3**, 86, **87**
  definition **55**, 77, **87**
refunds 113, 115
regulations 134, 135
religious discrimination 85
remittance advice slips 61–2, **62**, 63
rent 68, 69, 72
repair 72
reports 29, 31
reprographics 14
reputation 7
research and development 94
reserves 66, **67**
resources 56, 90–1
responsibility, at work 84–5
restaurant industry 110
retailers 128–9, **129**
retention 80–1
revenue 16, 56–9, **57**
rights, at work 84–5, 132, 133, 136
ringtones 112
risk 3, **3**, 36, 37, 38
Royal Mail 33
royalties 42, **43**

safety 114, 115, 133
  see also health and safety
Sainsbury's 128
salaries 25, 52, 72, 78, **79**
sales
  cost of 68, 69, **69**
  ethical 132, 133
  maximising 6, 73
  see also marketing and sales
sales invoices 60–1, **62**, 63
sales people 104
sales revenue 16, 25, 56
  definition **17**, **69**
  increasing 72
  on the profit and loss account 68, 69
security 15, 33
selection process 80, **81**
services 36, **37**, 138
shareholders 40, 67
shares 40, 40–1, **41**, 44, 54
Shell 44
shipbuilding 97
shops 129
short-lists 82, **83**
sick pay 77, **77**
single currency 136, **137**
single market 136, **137**
slogans 126, **127**
small businesses 16, 17
SMART objectives 7
Smith, Will 82
software 32, **33**
sole traders 36–7, **37**, 42, 44–5
  liability status 36, **37**, 40
  marketing and sales 104
  profit and loss accounts 68
  raising finances 54
Sony 134
span of control 13, **13**
spider diagrams (mind maps) 29
spreadsheets 32–3
staff discounts 78–9
stakeholders 2, **3**, 8–9
  external 8, **9**
  internal 8, **9**
standard of living 24
Starbucks 44, 72
starting a business 2–3
  business failure 2–3
  reasons for 2
  start-up grants 134, **135**
statements of account 62, **62**, 63
statistical process control 100, **101**
status 24, **25**
steel 97
stock 71, 92
  control 99
  costs 56, 72
stock exchange 41
strategic decision making 26, **27**
strike action 86, **87**
subsidiaries 45, **45**
Sudan 1 94, 95
supply 8, 128
survival 7
SWOT analysis 107, **107**

tactical decision making 26, **27**
take-overs 18, **19**, 40
tax returns 31

taxation 46, 52, 69, 134
technological change 76, 86, 99, 119
telephone calls 30
Tesco 128
tobacco companies 73
total quality management (TQM) 101, **101**
trade
  invisible 138, **139**
  overseas 136–7, 138–9
  visible 138, **139**
trade credit 55
trade unions 78, 86, **87**
training 76, 79, 80–1
  assistance with 97
  costs 72
  induction 81, **81**
  on rights and responsibility at work 84
transport 42, 72, 79
Transport for London 46
turnover 6, **7**

Unilever 118, 138
Unison 78
utilities 72

value added 90, **91**, 122, 123
vertical integration 18–19, **19**
  backwards 19
  forwards 18–19
video recorders 120
Virgin 36, 45
visible trade 138, **139**
vision statements 6
Vodafone 80
voluntary groups 48–9

wages 24–5, 52, 68–9, 72
  definition 78, **79**
  minimum 86, 136
wages clerks 53
Wal-Mart 18
waste
  disposal of 133
  measurement 98, 99
watchdogs 46, **47**, 134, **135**
water 72
Watson Burton 38
wholesalers 128, **129**
Wippit 112
word processing 14, 32, 33
word-of-mouth 110, **111**
worker co-ops 48, **49**
workers
  and costs 56
  and industry location 96
  motivating 24–5
  and production 92, 94, 95
  and productivity 98, 99
  and quality of production 101
working hours 136
working to rule 86
writers 104
written communication 30, 31
  see also letters

Xansa 84